TALIESIN

Recovering the poetic self

Horst Kornberger

First published 2017 by
INTEGRAL ARTS PRESS
PO Box 456 Hamilton Hill WA 6963
www.horstkornberger.com

Edited by Janet Blagg,
Design by Horst Kornberger
Cover image: Horst Kornberger
Produced by the Integral Arts Press

ISBN-13: 978-0-9802931-8-0

ISBN-10: 0-9802931-8-9

To the poets of the future

CONTENTS

ACKNOWLEDGMENTS

Thanks to storyteller Jenny Hill who brought this story to my attention and to the many workshop and course participants who have directly or indirectly contributed towards this book. Thanks to those who have generously allowed me to include their work. To Jennifer Kornberger for advice, support and encouragement and to Liana Christensen for additional contributions. And to my editor Janet Blagg who has again given generously of her time and expertise.

INTRODUCTION

This book is based on the Celtic tale of Taliesin, which I came across when I was developing my first creative writing course, *The Writer's Passage*. It was the right story at the right time as it contained in miniature what I was trying to achieve at large: a process for poetic empowerment.

Using this story as a catapult, beginners quickly gained imaginative capabilities, often creating pieces they never thought themselves capable of. Seasoned writers found it an effective recharge, and poets stuck in creative doldrums felt a fresh wind turning their pages.

The reason for this singularly potent effect is that the tale describes the archetypal process of becoming a poet.

'Poet', it should be said, meant something different in Taliesin's time. The word pointed towards the teacher, healer, adviser, mediator, visionary, word-smith, story-maker and magician of the Celtic world: the real rather than the nominal leader of the times.

Today, poetry is typically viewed as merely a personal pursuit: an intellectual pastime for some, a repository of endangered feelings for others; it has become peripheral rather than central, the icing on the cake rather than the leaven that makes it rise.

Or has it? The imagination, which is the core ingredient of poetic work, is becoming increasingly important in almost all spheres of life. We draw on it when we become teachers to our children, coffee-table therapists to friends, counsellors to colleagues; we apply it when we turn into innovators in our lives and visionaries in our professions. If you are a writer the imagination will lend you vivid description, poetry, plot, story; if you are an innovator it will point you toward new ideas; if you are a leader it will inspire constructive vision; if you are a psychologist it will endow you with therapeutic insights and pictures that heal.

So this book is written not only for poets and writers, but for everyone who wishes to develop their imagination.

It's a book to be worked with, a hands-on manual to develop poetic capability. The tale and its meaning will unfold in parallel with the exercises.

To make the most of this book I recommend that you step outside of your twenty-first century personality as well as many of your modern and post-modern convictions. For the time being immerse yourself in the tale and the way it is presented: as an imagination.

DAY ONE

The Preparation

There are six parts to the process. The first part is the preparation, which helps you to become aware of how prepared you already are.

The fact that you have picked up this book testifies that there is a poet in you. This is important as you cannot become a poet unless you already are one. The alchemists held that you needed gold to make gold, and the same applies to poetry. Luckily almost everyone has a thread of poetic gold woven through their life. By 'poetic' I do not mean verse on a page, but every experience that breaks you from the mould of convention, liberates you to greater intensity of feeling and reveals meanings usually unnoticed.

It you have ever been lifted by a play or transported by a piece of music then you have had such an experience. If you have been moved by a landscape, if your turbulent emotions have been levelled by a calm lake, or your own horizons widened at the sight of a vast plain then you have had this experience too. Epiphanies large and small: the comfort of returning to a well cleaned kitchen, the gaze of a newborn, dust motes suspended in the afternoon light, children playing with such abandon that you forget your own cares, and the momentous entry of love in your life all point towards this experience.

Everyone has had experiences that allow them a glimpse into, as Wordsworth put it, the 'life of things'. These experiences do not lead everyone along the path to becoming a poet, but they point the way. As you are reading this book I will assume you want to be a poet (or you consider yourself one), so we will start by gathering the experiences you already have. You can then evaluate them for what they are: signposts of the poetic, footprints that the poet in you has left for you to follow. Now is the time to revisit these footprints, discern their direction and start the journey.

Exercise 1 The body-poetic

Make a list of as many poetic experiences in your life as you can recall. Allow this some time. You are literally re-membering your body-poetic. I suggest you leave some space after this exercise as more memories may want to file in later. If you cannot think of any such experiences in your life, or can't remember them, invent some – this may help to have them in the future. Give each a short title – a name – as if it were the title of a poem. Here are some examples:

> *The tree that followed me around.*
> *Three ways to stay at home*
> *The colour of conversation*
> *The tug of Earth*

Exercise 2 Re-membering

Now take one of your titles and elaborate on it in a piece of writing. Do this by remembering the feeling, the atmosphere and the specific circumstances that contributed to the occasion. Contemplate what this experience has meant to you, how it has woven itself into the fabric of your life. If your memories are lean, fatten them with your imagination. If they are non-existent, I invite you to make them up. Write at least a paragraph, or use a poetic form, as in the example below.

The Tug of Earth
my mind jagged
a jungle of fears
body tight
a corkscrew

I take my shoes off
walk on prickly grass
pine needles broken shells
bring me to my feet
to the tug of earth
to body's refuge

the cry of Carnabies
low over pines
lifts me skyward

my thoughts now like clouds
dissolve into blue air
Annette Mullumby

Encounters with Poetry

The next step is to explore your encounters with poetry and literature, the moments when you were touched by words and uplifted by a well-wrought phrase. A story may have given you some new insight, a novel influenced your career or a poem changed the way you lived your life.

Exercise 3 Literary lifelines

Ask yourself: What is my favourite story? Which myths have been most meaningful to me? Who are my favourite poets and writers? Who was my favourite poet or writer when I was ten, twenty or thirty years old? And then make a list of poems, books, stories, plays and myths that have most influenced your life and arrange them in a timeline if you can (there is no need to be exact). You could start with a random list before attempting any order in time.

> *The Yearling - Marjorie Kinnan Rawlings.*
> *The Secret Garden - Frances Hodgson Burnett.*
> *The epic 'Roots' - Alex Haley*
> *The story of Siddhartha - Hermann Hesse*
> *The poetry of Mary Oliver*
> *The poetry of Yeats - especially The Lake Isle of Innisfree.*
> *The writings of John O'Donohue*
> *Winnie the Pooh*
> *Leunig cartoons*
> *Wild - Cheryl Strayed (especially the section where the mother is dying).*
> **Janet Paterson**

Once you have completed your list consider how these works have influenced you. What did they mean at the time? What have they meant since and what is their meaning now? Have they been catalysts and given you direction? Does the sequence tell a story? Is your life paralleled by the books you have loved? Can you see your literary hit list as an encrypted alphabet, as timely advice your poetic self has bestowed on your ordinary personality?

Exercise 5 Entitlements
Now create a poetic title that captures your relationship to each of the works on your list. Here are some examples:

Two ways, one road
When I was Sinbad the Sailor
 Homer on holiday
The page that turned my life

How I grew new hands
The poem that pursued me
How I lost myself in one book and found myself in another
No one knew it, not even myself

Exercise 5 Elaboration

Chose the title you like best and write about the experience. Allow the mood of your title to lead you.

How I grew new hands

The Handless Maiden was my favourite folktale. I was shocked by the images: a miserable father who sacrifices his daughter's hands so he can live, a betrayal by a messenger, new hands that grow back like a set of second teeth. I clearly saw the new hands budding out of the stumps of her arms and every time I pictured this I felt a jolt of strength. The physicality of the metaphor was potent. It was the first time that I experienced the healing power of an image, even one with a gruesome aspect.
Genevieve Arden

If you work with a partner or in a group share and discuss your poetic timeline.

Poetic Calling

Now it is time to remember the moment when you realised you had a destiny with words, when you first felt the longing to express yourself in poetry or prose.

The Chilean poet *Pablo Neruda* vividly remembers this moment:

And it was at that age ... Poetry arrived
in search of me. I don't know, I don't know where

it came from, from winter or a river.
I don't know how or when,
no they were not voices, they were not
words, nor silence,
but from a street I was summoned,
from the branches of night,
abruptly from the others,
among violent fires
or returning alone,
there I was without a face
and it touched me.

I did not know what to say, my mouth
had no way
with names,
my eyes were blind,
and something started in my soul,
fever or forgotten wings,
and I made my own way,
deciphering
that fire,
and I wrote the first faint line,
faint, without substance, pure
nonsense,
pure wisdom
of someone who knows nothing,
and suddenly I saw
the heavens
unfastened
and open,
planets,
palpitating plantations,
shadow perforated,
riddled

with arrows, fire and flowers,
the winding night, the universe.

And I, infinitesimal being,
drunk with the great starry
void,
likeness, image of
mystery,
felt myself a pure part
of the abyss,
I wheeled with the stars,
my heart broke loose on the wind.

Not every calling, of course is as definite and dramatic. *Margaret Atwood* recalls her poetic emergence in a very different way:

The day I became a poet was a sunny day of no great moment. I was scuttling along across the football field in my usual furtive way, suspecting no ill, when a large invisible thumb descended from the sky and pressed down on the top of my head. A poem formed. It was quite a gloomy poem: the poems of the young usually are. It was a gift, this poem – a gift from an anonymous donor and, as such, both exciting and sinister at the same time.

Callings can be subtle, can even go unnoticed: a poetic dawn that can take months, years or even decades.

Exercise 6 Re-awakening

Take some time and ponder your poetic, artistic, creative awakening.

What was it like? How old were you? Where were you? How did your interior word-worker announce him or herself? How did it feel? What did you make of it? Did you take your gift seriously? Did you begin writing straight away? And if so did you hide your productions or announce them with confidence. Or did it take time to come to terms with your new found ability?

Capture that first awakening to your creative self in a poem or piece of writing. As before, if you cannot remember, write as if you did. If you are sure that this has never happened to you and you are reading this book because you are hoping that it will, write about that hope, that longing, that wish. When did it start? And how did it feel when it started? And why are you following it now?

> A wordless poem arrived when I was seventeen years old. Wordless at the start because it announced itself on some invisible barometer as a change in weather. It was as if a pressure system was developing, a smallchaos near my torso, not inside but next to me, and it was asking something, breathing its little foreign wind into my lungs. It was a foundling who had decided it belonged to me. I was to give its inchoate existence a shape of words, tease out its images and in doing so bring relief to it.   .
> **Jennifer Kornberger**

Exercise 7 Read the Tale of Taliesin

The final exercise for day one is to read the tale in its entirety. It will not take you long. I recommend that you read the whole story and then let some time pass before commencing with the exercises that follow. Night is a great teacher and much soul-work happens while we are asleep.

Approach the tale with respect, without judgement or modern sentiments. Take the story as a metaphorical account of poetic initiation.

The Tale of Taliesin

There was once a sorceress whose name was Ceridwen. She ruled a great estate and was renowned for her powers of magic and knowledge. Ceridwen's only worry was her ill-favoured son Morfred, who was not only ugly but doltish.

To improve his prospects, Ceridwen set out to brew the cauldron of inspiration. Whoever was first to drink from this cauldron would become the greatest of bards, and gain the knowledge of all ages.

It took a year to make this brew. To keep the cauldron boiling Ceridwen employed Gwion, a handsome youth, to tend the fire and stir the broth while she was gathering rare herbs from near and far.

On the last day of the year Ceridwen went out once more to gather herbs. She ordered Gwion to stoke the fire more fiercely and stir the broth more strongly than ever before. And Gwion stoked the fire and stirred the broth with all his might. Soon the cauldron boiled and hissed so furiously that a drop of hot broth spurted onto Gwion's thumb. He cried out in pain and stuck his thumb into his mouth.

Now at that moment all the knowledge and skill prepared for Morfred poured into Gwion. Suddenly he knew everything there was to know. And because he knew everything he also knew that Ceridwen would seek revenge.

So he fled from his mistress' hall. But Ceridwen already knew by means of her art what had happened and was after him immediately.

Gwion ran as fast as he could. But no matter how fast he ran, Ceridwen ran faster. When he felt her coming closer and closer, Gwion used his newfound powers and changed himself into a hare. But Ceridwen changed herself into a greyhound. And as fast as he ran, she ran faster.

When Gwion came to a river, he jumped into it and changed

17

himself into a salmon. But Ceridwen jumped after him and became an otter. And as fast as he swam, she swam faster.

Gwion made a leap out of the water and changed himself into a raven and flew away. But Ceridwen changed herself into a falcon. And as fast as he flew, she flew faster.

On and on it went. Each time Gwion changed himself, Ceridwen changed herself too. And each time she came closer. When she was almost upon him Gwion slipped into a granary. He turned himself into one grain of wheat and hid himself in the large pile. But Ceridwen was not to be fooled. She changed herself into a speckled hen, looked around, scratched and searched until she spotted the grain that was Gwion, and she pecked it up and ate it.

This, however, was not to be the end of Gwion. For Ceridwen soon found that she was heavy with child. And as she had not lain with any man, she knew that this child could be no other than Gwion. She and Morfred decided to kill the babe as soon as it was born.

But it so happened that on the very day that Ceridwen gave birth, Morfred was out hunting. When Ceridwen saw the babe, he was so beautiful that she could not do what she had planned. So she made a leather bag, sealed it with wax, put the babe inside and set it adrift on the sea. There it floated for three days and three nights. And on the fourth day, which was Mayday, the bag washed up against the weir of king Gwyddo.

Now this king Gwyddo had an only son called Elphin, who was a needy and most unlucky youth. Misfortune followed him wherever he went and his father was much concerned about his future. On this same day Gwyddo had sent Elphin to the weir because on the first day of May there was always an abundant catch of salmon. This will surely turn his ill luck, his father thought, for he cannot fail to make a great catch.

But it was not to be. All day long the young prince cast his nets. And all day long he hauled in nothing but weeds. Not even one salmon was caught.

'Thou hast never been as unlucky as today', his attendants said, 'for now thou hast ruined the luck of this weir.'

It was already getting late and Elphin had given up hope. Yet he tried one more time. He cast his net as wide as he could and slowly hauled it in. Suddenly he felt a tug and he drew the net in with a will. But instead of a salmon he had caught a leather bag. Curious about his catch Elphin opened the bundle.

When he saw the beautiful babe inside, he cried out: 'Taliesin', which in Welsh means Radiant Brow. And the babe replied 'Yes, Taliesin is my name!'
Awed to hear a babe speak, Elphin, cried out:
'How is it that someone so small can speak so well?'
And to this Taliesin replied:

> Once I was a handsome youth
> Tutored in the hall of Ceridwen,
> And though of modest means
> I was great in her hall
>
> I was held in servitude
> Yet inspiration set me free.
> Learned I grew in ancient laws
> And in the speech before words.
>
> For the wisdom I gained
> I fled from her hall
> And shifted my shape.
>
> Since then
> I have been a hare
> Running in fright,
> A salmon swimming upstream,
> And a raven
> Of prophetic speech.

I have been a roe-buck
Leaping over hedges
A cunning fox, a sure swift
And a squirrel hiding in vain.

I have been iron
Hammered in fire,
The keen edge of a sword
And the cry in the midst of battle

I have been a struggling bull,
A bristling boar in a ravine,
I have been a grain of wheat,
Was eaten and born again.

I was laid in a bag
And floated on the waters,
But by happy omen
And God's will
I have come to light again.

Elphin was awed by what he heard and he took the boy tenderly in
his arms, and with a heavy heart returned to his father.

Taliesin however, knowing the prince's sorrow, began to sing
another song:

Fair Elphin, do not lament your fate
No catch at Gwyddo's weir
Was ever as good as today.

Dry your cheeks fair Elphin
For nothing is gained by sorrows.
Although you think yourself cheated
Your gain will be greater than your loss,

Though I am small
I am large in ability,
Though I am helpless now
I will bring help in time.

Fair Elphin, of generous mind,
Do not grieve any more
Though I was spumed
by Dylan's wave
I shall profit you more
Than all the salmon ever caught
At your father's weir.

Though I lie tied in a basket
There are wonders on my tongue,
And harm shall avoid you
When I am at your side.

Hearing this Elphin was much comforted and returned in high spirits. When King Gwyddo saw Elphin approach with his head held high he was pleased and thought that his son's luck had improved. 'How many salmon have you caught today', called out the king. And Elphin, glad about his haul, replied:
'I have caught something better than salmon!'
'And what might that be?' asked the king.
'I have caught a bard', Elphin replied, and held up the babe for all to see.
'A poet?' cried the king in dismay. 'What will a poet profit you?'
But before Elphin could reply, Taliesin answered in his stead.
'I will profit him more than all the salmon ever caught at your weir have profited thee.'
The king, greatly surprised to hear a small babe speak, said:
'Art thou so small a babe and so great a speaker?'
And to that Taliesin replied:

> I can speak better
> Than thou canst hear,
> Give more answers
> Than thou hast questions to ask.

'What or who are you?' asked the king. And Taliesin answered him in the way that poets do, with a song:

> From the vast waters I came
> With blessings great.

> I am thrice born
> And know by meditation
> What was and will be.

> I am versed in all sciences
> I can read the ciphers of the stars.

> I know the voices of the wind,
> and the true names of trees.

> I understand the tongue of the river
> And the seven languages of the sea.

The king and his court listened in awe and Elphin was glad about his haul. He gave his catch to his wife, who cared for him with great love.

From that time on all went well with Elphin. Ill luck ceased to knock on his door and good fortune entered instead. And the king and his court were mightily pleased.

Whenever there were questions, Taliesin knew the answer. When there was need, Taliesin found help. When there was conflict Taliesin helped with counsel. When there was sorrow Taliesin knew how to comfort. And whenever there was feasting (and there was much feasting at these times) Taliesin sang his songs.

So all went well and when his father died, Elphin became king. And with Taliesin at his side he and his kingdom prospered.

Now it so happened when Taliesin was thirteen years of age that Elphin was summoned to appear at the court of the high king, his uncle Maelgwyn. Elphin was slow to go as Maelgwyn was renowned for his pride and ill temper. But it was his duty to attend.

When he arrived he found the court just as pernicious as rumours had told. The king was surrounded by courtiers and bards employed to praise him and all that he possessed.

When at a feast one of the courtiers praised all the halls Maelgwyn possessed and land all the land owned, Elphin kept quiet. But when the same courtiers praised Maelgwyn's queen as by far the fairest and most virtuous, and the king's bard Heinin Vard, as by far the best singer of the land, Elphin could not hold his tongue. He replied that his wife was just as fair and virtuous a queen and that his own bard, Taliesin, was better than any other poet alive.

When this speech reached Maelgwyn's ears, he was greatly angered. He called his guards and had Elphin put in silver chains and thrown into the dungeon.

Then he called his son Rhun, a lecherous young man from whom neither maiden nor wife was safe. He sent him to Elphin's court to bring disgrace upon his nephew's wife. This task was much to Rhun's liking and he made haste.

Taliesin, however, who had stayed back with his foster mother, knew by his art of Rhun's intent. He warned the queen and advised her to change her apparel with that of her kitchen maid. And so the queen gave her rich clothes, necklaces and rings to the maid.

When Rhun arrived, Taliesin led him to a richly laid table. There he dined with the maid who was pretending to be queen. Secure in his luck Rhun drank much and made the kitchen maid drink likewise.

To hasten his errand he mixed a sleeping potion into the maid's wine. She soon fell asleep. Rhun carried her to his room and tried to slip her ring from her finger as a token of his success. But the ring was stuck on her plump finger and could not be removed. Rhun, impatient to return to his father's court, took his knife and cut off the finger. He then slipped away before daybreak.

Maelgwyn was greatly pleased when he saw his son bring back a token of success. He had Elphin brought before him and chided him because of his boast: Know that it was but your folly that made you trust the virtues of your wife. Here, behold her finger with your ring upon it. Rhun cut it off when she lay next to him drunk.

Elphin took one look at the ring on the finger and replied undaunted, 'There is no doubt that the ring on the finger is the ring of my wife. But there is also no doubt that the finger inside the ring is not that of my queen. Look for yourself. This is not the fair, slim finger of a queen, but the rough finger of a maid that cleans the kitchen and kneads the dough.'

The king and his courtiers looked closely. When they saw the dough in the fingernail, they all agreed that this was not the finger of a queen, but that of a kitchen maid.

Maelgwyn, however, became even angrier than before.

'Be that as it may', he cried, 'you will not go from here until you have proved that your bard is better than mine. Take him back to the dungeon!'

So Elphin sent messengers to Taliesin and asked him to come and prove his skills before the king and his court. But long before they arrived Taliesin was already on his way. Before he left, his foster mother asked him, 'How will you free my husband?' And Taliesin answered, as he usually did, with a song:

I will go on my journey
Until I come to the gate
Of Maelgwyn, the king.

I will enter his hall
And silence the bards

I will humble the proud,
Undo the poets
Who ply their craft
For wicked ends,
The singers of false songs
And makers of evil schemes.

I Taliesin, chief of the bards
Will free fair Elphin
From his silver chains,
I will revenge my master
On Maelgwyn the High King
And his lecherous son,.

Their lives shall be short
And their lands laid to waste.

Taliesin arrived at the king's castle long before he was expected. It so happened that on that day the king had ordered a great feast. Among the many arrivals no one noticed the young bard who sat himself quietly in the corner of the hall.

Soon the king arrived, followed by his courtiers and a bevy of bards ready to sing Maelgwyn's praise. As the bards passed by Taliesin, he pouted his lips, and when they began their singing all they could do was mumble. Maelgwyn rose in anger and had the master bard Heinin Vard brought before him; but he too could only mumble and point to the young boy in the corner who had spellbound his speech.

The king turned towards Taliesin and asked him who he was and why he had vexed the bards of the court. And Taliesin answered the king with this verse:

I am Taliesin,
Chief bard I am to Elphin
And the summer stars are my home,
Once I was called Merlin
But now I am known as Taliesin.

I was in the heavens
When Lucifer fell to the depths,
I bore the banner before Alexander
I know the stars in North and South
I was in Canaan when Absalom was slain
I was in the court of Don before the birth of Gwdion
I have been a year and a day in the fortress of Arianrod
I was loquacious before I was gifted with speech
I witnessed the destruction of Sodom and Gomorrah
I was the architect of Nimrod's tower
I was in India before the building of Rome
I upheld Moses in the waters of Egypt,
I have been under the cross with Mary Magdalen,
I have received the Muse from Ceridwen's cauldron,
I have been bard to Lleon of Lochlin
I have been on the White Hill at the court of Cynvelyn,

I have been fostered in the lands of the deity,
I have taught all ages and instructed all spheres,
I shall remain until the last day of the world.

No one knows if my body is flesh or fish.
For nine months I was in the womb of Ceridwen,
Once I went by the name of Gwion
But now I have become Taliesin.

The king and his nobles marvelled greatly at his song. For never
had they heard anybody sing with such skill. The king then ordered

Heinin Vard, his master bard, to frame a reply. But Heinin could do
nothing but mumble.

Seeing that his bards were of no avail, the king asked Taliesin
what his errand was. The bard replied:

I have come to measure myself
Against the king's bards,
To win back my lord Elphin
From the belly of the tower
And loosen the chains that hold him
Prisoner in this place.

Then Taliesin turned to Maelgwyn's bards and rebuked them with
a song.

If you were bards
You would know the mysteries
And declare them to the world.

If you were bards
You would know the terrible beast
Rising from the abyss,
The obnoxious creature
Who rules the shallows and the deep

If you were bards
You would know him
Whose jaws are wide as mountains
Whom neither weapons
Nor strength will subdue,
The one with the ice cold eye
In his head.

If you were bards
You would know
Falsehood from truth
And tell your king
Of the terrible creature

That will come from the sea-marsh
To devour him and his kin.

Yet in spite of Taliesin's warning, the king was still unwilling to let
his nephew go. So Taliesin commenced a song about the wind:

Know thou the strong one
From before the flood;
Without flesh, without bone,
Without vein, without blood,
Without hands, without feet
Who will not be older or younger
Than when he began.

The sea pales
When he approaches,
Great are his gusts
When he comes from the south,
White foam stirs
When he strikes from the coast.
Without hand without foot
Without youth, without age
He was never born
And never grows old.

He is as wide as the earth
He will not come when desired
Nor leave when asked
His course is unknown,
He is indispensable
He is without equal
He is four-sided;
He is unfettered
He is incomparable;
He will not be advised,
He commences his journey
Above the high rocks

He is sonorous, he is dumb
He is mild, he is strong,
He is bold
When he glances over the land,
He is clamorous,
On the face of the earth.

He will destroy
But not repair the injury;
He is wet, he is dry,
He commences his course
From the heat of the sun,
And the cold of the moon.

Among all beings
One has prepared him
To wreak vengeance
On Maelgwyn, the King.

When he began singing a breeze began to stir. The breeze turned
into a wind and the wind into a storm. Soon the storm raged so
furiously that Maelgwyn thought that the walls of his stronghold
might break. He quickly sent his guards to fetch his nephew. As
soon as Elphin arrived Taliesin sang a song that loosened the silver
chains from his limbs. Then he sang another song in praise of all
bards who stand by their calling:

What was the first man
Made by the Gods;
What was his speech
What was his meat, what his drink,
What roof his shelter;
What his first sight
What the first thought
Of his thinking;
What the clothing;
That covered his form.

Wherefore should a stone be hard;
Why should a thorn be sharp-pointed?
Who is hard like a flint;
Who is salt like brine;
Who is sweet like honey;
Who rides on the gale;

Why is the nose straight;
Why is the wheel round;
Why is the tongue gifted with speech;

If thy bards, Heinin, be competent,
Let them reply to me, Taliesin.

The king's bards hung their heads and none dared reply. Thus the contest was finally won and Elphin freed. Right glad was Taliesin and right glad was Elphin, his master.

This ends day one. Don't forget to let at least one night pass before you begin work on the exercises for day two.

DAY TWO

How to approach the tale

I suggest you take this tale as an account of events that were real to those who experienced them at a time when inner and outer realities overlapped.

Taliesin is the Welsh name for Merlin, which in turn was the generic name for the master druid of the Celts, a name which later became the title bestowed on those who achieved the same rank. The story is ancient and has changed much over time, nevertheless the central motifs can still be glimpsed under layers of later lore. Ceridwen, for instance, appears in some tales as a sorceress, in others a witch. But under the hag mask of later times hides an earlier goddess who bestowed poetic skill and knowledge. This was the goddess who brewed the cauldron of inspiration and initiated the bardic druids.

For the poet-apprentice today it is important to realise that what in former ages was experienced externally, in later times becomes internalised. This means that today there is a Taliesin in every poet and writer. There is also an unlucky Elphin, a conventional Gwyddo, an overbearing Maelgwyn, a lecherous Rhun, a trustworthy queen and a gullible maid in all of us. There are also, particularly in those aspiring to become poets, any number of false bards ready to sing shallow praises for the sake of convenience. And there is, of course, Ceridwen, ready to bestow poetic initiation on those who seek it.

Entering the tale

Now we are going to revisit the story in stages, stopping to introduce exercises where appropriate. I suggest you do the exercises as they arise, without reading ahead. Don't think about them. Simply do them. Stay in the moment, trust the process and your imagination will do the work for you. Think in pictures if you can. If you can't, write as if you could. Whatever happens, do not censor yourself while you write. Approach the exercises in the spirit of play and let yourself be surprised.

Let's begin by once more wrapping the cloak of story around us. As I retell the tale, imagine what you hear as a movie projected onto the screen of your mind.

Imagine Gwion, the handsome youth apprenticed to Ceridwen. See him labouring ceaselessly in her great hall. He has served for a whole year and now the last day has come. He is stoking the fire and stirring the seething broth. A hot drop spurts unto his thumb and the bright light of poetic inspiration pours into him. In that moment he knows everything there is to know. And because he know everything he knows know that Ceridwen will seek revenge.

See him running from her hall, the goddess following apace. When he turns himselfself into a hare, she turns herself into a greyhound. When he slips away as a salmon she pursues as an otter, when he escapes as a raven she follows as a falcon. He becomes fox and frog, fire and iron. Again and again he changes shape, and again and again Ceridwen changes shape too. Desperate, Gwion turns yourself into a tiny grain and hides in large pile of wheat. Ceridwen becomes a hen and scratches until she finds Gwion and swallows him whole.

He enters the womb of poetic becoming. The goddess

becomes his mother. He becomes her son. Her gifts become his. He is born, put in a casket, set on the rocking sea. He floats on the waves and is hauled in by a net. The bag is opened and Elphin, inspired for the first time in his life, calls out his name. And Taliesin, aware of who he is, sings his first song. And this song tells us how he became a bard:

> I was held in servitude
> Yet inspiration set me free.
> Learned I grew in ancient laws
> And in the speech before words.

You have to become familiar with this *speech before words* before you too can become a bard.

The Life of Language

To be acquainted with the laws of language and speech was crucial for the poets of the past. Today it is even more important as we have lost conscious relationship with language as language, with sound before it congeals into words and fixed meanings. To become aware of this realm we must look through words into that which precedes them.

Read aloud the following excerpt from *Gerard Manly Hopkins'* poem *Inversnaid* a few times until you feel the sounds tumbling over your teeth and tongue.

> This darksome burn, horseback brown,
> His rollrock highroad roaring down,
> In coop and in comb the fleece of his foam
> Flutes and low to the lake falls home.

Feel into the soundscape Hopkins creates. It is strikingly descriptive. The consonantal sequence of k – p and k – b in *coop* and *comb* invokes the boulders and rocks, and the repetition of f and l the quickly flowing, waters eventually calmed by the h–m of home at the end of the stanza. Throughout the poem the interplay of rhythm and consonants imitates various speeds and aspects of the brook, speaks in the language before words.

Hopkins' lines rely primarily on the descriptive effect of consonants. In the lines by *e.e cummings* below it is mood of the vowels that is of foremost importance.

> i thank you God for most this amazing day,
> for the leaping greenly spirits of trees
> and a blue true dream of sky ...

The bright, quick and exuberant 'eeh' sounds of the second line prick with intensity and life (there are seven of them!) The 'ooh' (as in blue and true) in the third line slows, calms and covers the nervous and overexcited 'eehs'. Note how the rhythms harmonise with the moods of the vowel-scapes. The second line gallops in heedless abandon while the third steadies itself with a trochee – the repetition of two or in this case three, long (emphasised) syllables blue – true – dream.

The Artwork of Words

The reason that language is so admirably onomatopoetic (able to imitate through sound) is that the words themselves have this capacity. You have to speak them, taste them, and listen into them to become aware of their undercover poesies. The word *meander* meanders as the river from which it derived its name. Speak the word *Lid*. Can you hear the lid being softly put on the pot with the final *d*?

The word canoe is a perfect replica of its shape. The sound 'k' is the wedge that cuts through the water and the rest of its slim form follows in its wake.

Can you hear the wave *wash* onto the *shore*. Can you feel the humming in the *m* of hum. Speak the word *thin* and observe how the already flattened breath that carries this word between tongue and teeth, becomes even thinner when *th* squeezes through the *n* of its end. *Thin.* It is hard to utter the word *smirking* without your facial features doing an unintended impersonation. A *thud* follows a fall with a dull, come down to earth 'd'. Can you hear the water tumble over *cataract* and glass break in *shattered*?

Explore the overlap of sound and meaning in words like: shimmering, shot, marmalade, malleable, cut, leap, fresh, dull, itchy and oil; compare thump and thumb, prickly and smooth, pop-up and balloon.

Exercise 1 Words that speak

Familiarise yourself with this hidden layer of language. Make a list of at least five onomatopoetic words. Then choose one or two and describe how the sound expresses meaning and in what way these word imitate in sound what they point to in concept.

Soundscapes

Words have the gift of portrayal because sounds have. Sounds are a kind of language, albeit one we have largely forgotten. Human beings all over the world use similar sounds for similar things. In older times this was an undisputed truth that underpinned the mantric use of language.

To master bards such as Taliesin, vowels and consonants were entities, beings, co-creators of reality: they had agency, power and impact beyond their subjection to words. Meaningful in and of themselves, sounds were experienced as manifestations of great archetypal gestures that ruled, formed and shaped the world. The world was experienced as divinely spoken. Nature was a poem made manifest. That poets, even if they are confirmed materialists like *Pablo Neruda*, never entirely lose sensitivity for the numinous dimension of sound, is revealed in the following passage:

...You can say anything you want, yessir, but it's the words that sing, they soar and descend ... I bow to them ... I love them, I cling to them, I run them down, I bite into them, I melt them down ... I love words so much ... The unexpected ones ... The ones I wait for greedily or stalk until, suddenly, they drop ...

Vowels I love ... They glitter like colored stones, they leap like silver fish, they are foam, thread, metal, dew ... I run after certain words ... They are so beautiful that I want to fit them all into my poem ... I catch them in mid-flight, as they buzz past, I trap them, clean them, peel them. I set myself in front of the dish. They have a crystalline texture to me, vibrant, ivory, vegetable, oily, like fruit, like algae, like agates, like olives ... And then I stir them, I shake them, I drink them, I gulp them down, I mash them, I garnish them, I let them go ... I leave them in my poem like stalactites, like slivers of polished wood, like coals, pickings from a shipwreck, gifts from the waves ...

Everything exists in the word ... An idea goes through a complete change because one word shifted its place, or because another settled down like a spoiled little thing inside a phrase...

Let us consider the nature of sounds. Take the consonant K and compare it with M. Speak them out loud and feel into their difference, their character and being. Start with K (as in keep, crumb or cut). K emanates a decisive, clear and cutting strength. M is a much softer, more nurturing, malleable, amiable sound. It readily appears in mum, mother, meander, malleable, mixture, more and mellifluous. It almost melds into the vowels while K pushes them rather coldly, unconcernedly and sometimes even violently into the world.

The letter W in wave even looks like a wave and has a similar quality. Just speak the word and watch the wave rolling through the 'w' until it washes with a 'v' flat onto the shore.

B builds, surround, forms, encompasses, provides skin and boundary like in boat, budding, baby, bowl. Of course, consonants will also appear in many words contrary to their obvious nature. Here they serve in subtler, less obvious ways.

The more you see sounds as beings, characters concocting the magical brew we call words, the more language will come alive in you. And the more it comes alive in you, the better you will write. A writer must become familiar with their qualities, with the formidable forces of vowels and consonants, and see them not as parts but as wholenesses in and of themselves. Not accidental occurrences that just happen to be in certain words, but creators, archetypes alive in the manifestation of sound, gods in the garb of vowels. This is the language before words.

Exercise 2 Consonants

Take a consonant such as B, L, K, M, N, S, and without much thinking let this consonant tumble onto your page, forming words whose sequences may or may not mean anything. The important thing is to experience the particular intent and momentum of an M or a K, how they want to form cadences and sentences of their own accord, be spoken in certain ways and with certain dynamics. Try a word-tumble, in which you spill out words, allowing sense or nonsense to spontaneously arise. Feel words impelled by words, sound created by sounds. If you have never considered sound on its own before, consider it now. If you have not loved consonants, make this exercise your first approach and courtship. Abandon your need to make sense and enjoy language for language's sake.

> *Word tumble for R*
> *more gore sore tor lore store*
> *forevermore restrict restrain*
> *resist wrestle wrangle relax*
> *resounding ruth ruthless*

revel in the restless time
revelation and book of Revelations,
the Resistance
are garner learn rare
radar
residual resident
now join our revels
stars responsible resume
resume remember relinquish
relay and comprise
Patricia Johnson

G word tumble
Grrrrrrrrrrr, growl, giddyup. Goddamn galahs;
it's 5 o'clock in the morning – gooooooo away!
Good God! what a gorgeous sunrise.
Get up, gallop, go forth with great gumption.
Nan Maria

Repeat the exercise with as many consonants as you like. You will find it enlivening and liberating.

Exercise 3 Vowels

Now try the same with the vowels a, e, i, o, u. Choose three vowels to work with and explore the quality and the mood of their soundscape. Write one line for each vowel. The vowel 'eeh' (as in peel) will incline you to a different language speed than the vowel 'ooh' (as in doom). Forgo your need to create meaningful sentences. Allow the vowel to lead you and let your pen follow in its wake. Write in the spirit of play. For example:

Eel empty, entrance keel, feel forward eerily, meet Mexicans and seal instructors, seemingly eat air.

Dot or Dorothy Robbins, domiciled in a sob, seldom at opera or olden rock concerts, obtuse to the point of snob.

Exercise 4 Soundscapes unlimited

Now write a longer piece that allows vowels and consonants to freely play with one another, without you superimposing the rules. Let your writing be carried by the momentum of sounds and savour their accidental combinations. Feel that sound has a will of its own and follow its intent.

> *Hrih Hrih Hrih*
> *a aa ahhhh*
> *o o o*
> *ooo ooo ooo*
> *B B B Butt Butting Buttress*
> *Buxom Bum Bumptious Bollocks*
> *Beautiful*
> *p p p puff put pigeon, pat paw press prayer*
> *Hello, Hi Hi How Hoo*
> *Ha ha Ha Hum Hum Hum*
> *Ma ma Mama Mother More most*
> *man moon monkey money*
> *queer quokka quick choir*
> *soft sing sung soul sum*
> *see saw sound soothe*
> *ache aim ail aid*
> *a a antelope amber accident*
> *attitude apple*
> *Tam ta Tum ta*
> *tea tog talk tittle tattle tall*
> *tree trunk trawl*
> right raw round rich ra rah!
> *Ra rolling ruckus raucous needy now number numb*
> *nada, no, No, nick, nock*
> *Nothing, Naaa*
> *Yes! Yay! Yah! yoo -yo!*
> *Ah   ah   aaaah ....*
> **Bev Barker**

39

Poetic Memories

Taliesin tells us he has been a hare, a salmon, a raven, a swift, a boar, a hot iron, a battle cry and a grain of wheat. For most of us such recollections are out of the range of possibility. The bard's pre-birth experience is a form of memory reserved for those

> ... *Who, from the womb, remembered the soul's history*
> *Through corridors of light, where the hours are suns,*
> *Endless and singing. Whose lovely ambition*
> *Was that their lips, still touched with fire,*
> *Should tell of the Spirit, clothed from head to foot in song*
> **Stephen Spender**, *The Truly Great.*

Some of us, and perhaps all of us if we look deeply enough, will have some faint recollection from very early childhood, or even before our birth. *William Wordsworth,* for whom this was still a tangible memory, has touched on this state and its inevitable loss in his poem, *Intimations of Immortality* from *Recollections of Early Childhood.*

> *There was a time when meadow, grove, and stream,*
> *The earth, and every common sight,*
> *To me did seem*
> *Apparelled in celestial light,*
> *The glory and the freshness of a dream.*
> *It is not now as it hath been of yore;—*
> *Turn wheresoe'er I may,*
> *By night or day.*
> *The things which I have seen I now can see no more.*

The poet's experience of childhood echoes what came before birth. Poets like Wordsworth typically keep a foot (or a toe) in the door of this universal childhood. They remember, though with less clarity, what Taliesin remembered. And because they remember, they try to manifest it in their writing.

Plato too speaks about the soul as omniscient before birth: then, as it leaves its true home and approaches the world of appearances, it drinks from the water of Lethe, the river of forgetfulness. Thus it exchanges omniscience for the limited knowledge of this world. Only the initiated can recover what others lose by coming into this world. They gain by dint of effort what Taliesin never forgot: a conscious connection to their trans-temporal being and the knowledge that being holds.

The Indian saint Yogananda described being conscious at birth in his 'Autobiography of a Yogi', and similar stories are told of Zarathustra and Buddha. Taliesin also remembered pre-birth universality, having been one with raven and fox, salmon and deer, spear point and sword edge. And like the Buddha, his memory becomes his first song.

At first sight this may all seem out of reach for contemporary writers. But what is beyond the ordinary personality is well within the ambit of the poetic self. For this self is part-Taliesin, a descendent of poetic ancestors that can be traced back to the first master bard. While fully realised memory may be out of reach, artistic awareness is at hand (particularly when that hand holds a pen attuned to the imagination).

In fact, this is what you will do in the next exercise. But first, read Taliesin's song again, this time as if it were your song. Don't skip it because you think you already know it. Read it out loud and with conviction. This is a poetic ritual in which repetition is essential. Take this song as a poetic mantra, an invocation of the muse.

> Once I was a handsome youth
> Tutored in the hall of Ceridwen,
> And though of modest means
> I was great in her hall
> I was held in servitude
> Yet inspiration set me free.
> Learned I grew in ancient laws
> And in the speech before words.

For the wisdom I gained
I fled from her hall
And shifted my shape.

Since then
I have been a hare
Running in fright,
A salmon swimming upstream,
And a raven
Of prophetic speech.

I have been a roe-buck
Leaping over hedges
A cunning fox, a sure swift
And a squirrel hiding in vain.

I have been iron
Hammered in fire,
The keen edge of a sword
And the cry in the midst of battle.

I have been a struggling bull,
A bristling boar in a ravine,
I have been a grain of wheat,
Was eaten and born again.

I was laid in a bag
And floated on the waters,
But by happy omen
And God's will
I have come to light again.

Exercise 5 Memories from before Birth

Now it is time to remember your experiences before you were born. What you cannot remember you can imagine, and that is just as well. You will become hare and raven, bear and boar.

Identify for the time being with Taliesin. Imagining being a great bard will help you to become one. Start by writing – and I suggest you write by hand to enhance the effect –

I am Taliesin

Then add at least five new examples of what you have been, writing each one out in full.

I am Taliesin
I have been a stag
I have been an otter
I have been a lean cow
I have been a solitary goldfish
I have been a fox foraging on the wood's edge
I have been a whale ploughing the Arctic sea.
I have been a snake of thorough understanding
I have been a bear caught in a cage of my fur

Whether you are working in a group or on your own, read out what you have written. Read as if called upon to reveal the truth.

Exercise 6 Variations

Now take one of the statements you have just written and vary it by repeating the beginning and changing the end of the line. Explore what kind of creature you have been with your variations. Always write the whole statement out each time.

I have been a whale ploughing the sea
I have been a whale spouting water

I have been a whale hunted to death
I have been a whale beached in a bay
I have been a white whale

or

I have been a lean cow drinking from a shallow stream
I have been a lean cow halting the traffic on an Indian street
I have been a lean cow grazing in a parched meadow
I have been a lean cow led to the slaughter-house

The Power of Imagery

Always use concrete, pictorial, imagery. Consider the following:

I have been a lean cow that did not know what to do

The second part – *'that did not know what to do'* – is a cold concept, information that disengages us from the concrete image of the lean cow. We lose sight of it standing there. We are forced to think, are made to understand rather than see. By contrast, when we are led to see the lean cow drinking from a shallow stream we become anchored in a picture that immediately engages more of our imagination. We see more of the cow standing, wading, waiting in a stream. We see it black or brown or brindled, or perhaps in muted white, maybe with its tail flicking and its warm, dark, moist nose beset by flies. We might elaborate the image by seeing other cows standing nearby, in the river and on the bank. We will inevitably see the stream winding or straight, the water clear or perturbed, the banks wooded or bare, pebbled, rocky, sandy or otherwise.

We will draw a landscape from a fragmentary line, place the shallow stream on a flat and fertile plain or amid sun burned hills. We will also, if ever so faintly and momentarily, want to migrate to India or Norway, experience the pampas or the prairies.

Using our imagination we put ourselves as well as the reader on the cliff edge of expectation. The intensity and detail of your imagery will depend on the state of your imagination. But no matter what state it is in (and it can always keep improving), it will have the propensity to make whole what is seen in part. It will add, piece out and elaborate what is already there.

The point I am making here is that while concepts tend to be fixed and finished, separate and isolating, the imagination remains alive. We are made active and participatory.

The distinction between image and concept, imagination and intellect, is important. Each has its function and both are powerful tools when applied in the right place. A good essay will depend on your ability to think clearly and weave your concepts into a comprehensive and well-structured whole. A good story draws on your ability to imagine vividly and let pictures unfold in your mind's eye. Good poetry and good writing will always employ both.

Today it is imagination we need most. Intellectuality we already have aplenty.

With this in mind examine the variations you wrote in exercise 6. Did you engage in pictures or concepts? Did you imagine or think, show or tell? If you have employed intellect rather than imagination, told rather than shown, rework your lines in the spirit of seeing rather than thinking. Read the results out loud and observe the effect – on yourself and on any listeners.

Exercise 7 Variation to momentum

Now repeat the exercise in the following way, drawing on what you have just learned without being overly conscious of it. Write another set of variations. Then, after a while, leave all repetition behind and allow the momentum gained to flow into a longer, free-formed piece.

> *I have been an ant following the trail.*
> *I have been an ant swarming over the ant-hill.*
> *I have been an ant picking a carcass clean.*

I have been an ant stopping for another.
I have been an ant carrying a crumb high overhead, back to the nest, my antennae tasting the air, six legs rattling, moving down the line,
No bigger than a grain, down into the tunnel; the clicking in my ears,
Over, under and through to the darkest place, there to feed the queen,
Spinning on my light legs, back into the light,
Embroidering the path with my brothers, rubbing antennae
And tasting, tasting the air for more.
Kevin Mazzer

I have been an old hand that collected old bones.
I have been an old hand that collected old bones, and washed the bones clean.
And laid them out.
Bone by bone.
I have been an old singing hand that sang over the bones under starlight.
I have been an old weeping hand in the rain that covered them over, bone by bone.
I have been a hand that prayed.
Gilly Berry

Exercise 8 Go direct

Now you have gained momentum you should be able to use it straight away. Take one of the lines you have written (or make up a new one) and launch immediately into description. If your line was about being a whale, describe how it was to be a whale ploughing the sea. Try not to think conceptually. Treat being a whale as a personal memory. Think in pictures the way we remember in pictures. Explore being a whale, tree, or cheetah, using all your senses.

Here are two examples:

I have been a wallaby in the bush by the sea.
Eyes scanning.
Ears twitching.
Nose filtering.
Head turning.
Hind feet ready.
Tail earthed.

I have heard waves crashing.
Seagulls crying.
People passing.
Trees groaning.

All the while;
Listening
Looking
Turning
Smelling

Sensing
Earth
Sky
Air

Nose divining; sweet green ahead
Earthed tail lifting
Hind feet propelling
Curled paws descending
Tongue protruding
Front teeth scissoring
Hind teeth grinding
Eyes scanning.
Ears twitching.
Nose filtering.
Head turning.
Hind feet ready.
Tail earthed.
Janet Paterson

I have been a cheetah, blood-drenched fangs sunk in the carcass of a wildebeest. The snapping crunch of cheetah's jaws on bone. The lifted head, the wary stance, controlled and silent tension rippling through skin and fur.

I've been that moment when the flying outstretched claws made contact, oh made contact with a lumbering, fleeing form and dragged it, screaming, to the ground. Deep pools of eyes that glow in darkening bush beneath a thorny tree.

I have been the cheetah's hunt, the bloody feast, and – on the grass there – the lolling empty eyes in severed skull; was live, is dead.

Sue Johnson

If your launch into creative action has failed to produce the results you hoped for, return to the previous exercise and vary your topic through a series of repetitions before exploring it. Use repetition as a crutch until you are able to walk without it.

Exercise 9 Trading lines

This exercise will liberate your writing from your usual choices, patterns and idiosyncrasies. We will attempt this by allowing a partner to provide you with a beginning line, so it is a line that you would not have chosen yourself. And you, in return, will provide a line for them.

Take the chance to leave your poetic comfort zone and venture into a more highly charged 'terra creativa.' This can be achieved by encouraging your partner to give you a challenging line or by choosing one of the more challenging examples provided below.

Do not be dismayed! In almost all cases a difficult, unattractive or challenging line yields superior results. Seemingly attractive topics such as dolphins and unicorns, roses, stars and sunsets are creativity traps. They are clichés that tend to create offspring in their image and likeness. They act on the reader like a favourite meal they have eaten so often they can't stand it anymore. It takes a master poet to make them appetising again. Apprentices had best avoid them altogether. The same applies to sentimentality, that deadly sweet syrup ready to drown any creative attempt. Good writing is courageous; fresh and daring, it is not achieved by leaning back in the armchair of convention.

Here are a few beginning lines of various intensity for those who are working with this book on their own.

I have been a falcon in free fall
I have been a rat in a rat hole
I have been a parrot in a cage

I have been a boar speared in a ravine
I have been a quagmire in a shallow stream
I have been the spittle dripping from a toothless mouth

And here are two examples from writers who have dared to enter challenging territory.

Shark
And then I became a shark.
Silent, Darting. Slicing.
Listening.
The flint of light in my glistening eye.
Looking.
Waiting.
With Teeth...
Ten thousand teeth.
Tiffany Gee

Yes, I have been a quagmire in a shallow stream. And yes, I growled and grumbled thickly through folds of mud. I shifted restlessly, I rose from deep dark caverns to the purple

surface. I sank and rolled and heaved and burbled, regurgitating the deepest contents of my belly. I sometimes looked for hapless wanderers, distracted by their thoughts, not watching where they trod, and I have grabbed their trembling ankles and slowly, relentlessly, pulled them down, deep down, to where I first was born – in the agony and dying trickle of a stream......
Sue Johnson

This ends day two. Wipe the mud from your pen and have a rest. You deserve it.

DAY THREE

Entering the Elements

Did you notice that Gwion's transformations went from hare (earth) to salmon (water) to raven (air)? Later he even became iron hammered in fire and the cry in the midst of battle (internal fire). This follows the druids' journey through the four elements – earth, water, air and fire. In the Celtic tradition participation in nature was an essential aspect in bardic initiation and the merging with the elements was its first step.

Four Elements

The idea of four elements was widespread. The notion of an element meant something different then. Today the name points to basic chemical building blocks; once it denoted states of matter and, simultaneously, of mind.

Earth was everything that was solid and separate: rocks, metals, a piece of driftwood, a cup, a blade or a grain of sand are certainly solid and therefore related to earth; a sand dune, on the other hand, being moveable and susceptible to the vagaries of weather and wind, was not.

Even seemingly solid iron will melt when heated. Heat it further and it will change into air and waft like gas. Pushed further it will return to the states of light and warmth from which it derived. In the time of Taliesin even light had two sides: an outer manifestation that illumines the things of this world and an inner one that sheds light on those things by means of thought.

All four elements possessed this double nature. Earth, for instance, was experienced in everything that is hard, rigid, finished, and unchangeable in the nature and in the soul. Clear thoughts and solid convictions are its positive expression, while obsession and rigidity take the negative pole. Water not only flowed in rivers but in the fluidity of language, air expanded in all forms of empathy and love, and fire, the cradle of all creation, kindled original thought.

Examine your writing so far. Have you gravitated towards a beast that lives on or even in the earth? Did fish and finned creatures enter your imagination? Or did you prefer swift winged birds? Have you dared inhabit a sword blade, a cauldron, a pot or the song of a maiden?

In the next exercise you will explore the four elements, either through the beasts that live in them or their qualities: the solidity of rock, the fluidity of water, the agile sensitivity of air and the fierce temper of fire.

Exercise 1 Elemental lines

Write four lines, each pertaining to one of the elements.

> *I have been a clod of earth*
> *I have been a moon jellyfish*
> *I have been a conch shell*
> *Yes, I have been a dragon breathing fire.*

Exercise 2 Earth

Now elaborate on your earth line. Remember what has been said about this element. Feel and sense yourself into it. Allow the poet in you to inhabit earth and try to let it inhabit you.

Earth (excerpt)
I have been a clod of earth, in a wide field, ploughed by two
black horses.
A clod turned over, wet and heaving.
Dissolved in rain.
Seeped deeper down beneath the surface.

I have been a clod, now silt, submerged.
I've tasted roots, an old gold coin, stones, buried wood, a
coffin with its body.
Gilly Berry

Water

'Water' means everything fluid: well water, river water, sea water, rainwater, tap water, blood, spittle and mucus, syrup and honey, oil and vinegar, quicksilver and sap in the bodies of plants. It was seen in molten metals, the flow of lava, the sluggish propulsion of tar and the even slower motion of glass.

Its presence was felt in the passing of time, the flow of music, the elegance of the dancer, the mobility of thought, the link between two concepts, the understanding before it is understood.

Water is a transformer that is itself constantly transformed. It gives and takes, dissolves and precipitates. Freeze it and it turns to earth, warm it and it wakes to air. Like our thinking it is ever malleable and takes any form or shape it is poured into. It is selfless, sensitive and receptive, a liquid instrument of the subtle imprints of planets and the obvious tug of the moon.

And water, of course, is the invisible life of plants. Plants only seem to be solid. Constantly in movement they are slow liquids rising in different speeds. Imagine a mighty oak, a gigantic jarrah, a dramatically gnarled olive tree as slow motion fountains rising and falling over centuries, and a snowdrop, a sunflower, or a spider orchid as a short-lived spring. To the degree you imagine this (rather than think it) you will water your mind.

Exercise 3 Water

Let all this inform what you write about water. You need not remember exact details; what matters is that you retain a feeling, a sense, a relationship to the element and thus invite it into your writing. Write with water and it will bring you into flow.

I have been a moon jellyfish

see through flesh
a fine fringe of filaments
sway scraps
to sucking mouth

tangles in weed
rocky waves
shove to shore
in sea spit ...
Annette Mullumby

Air

Water weighs. The air frees itself from such shackles. Led by levity it exists everywhere, expands on all sides, occupies all space, embraces all things, touches all surfaces, and fills every nook and crack with its spacious presence. It is quick, unattached, and notoriously sanguine. It moves easily and is easily moved.

Wedded to warmth and cold, air is swayed by the slightest change. Move a pen and you stir it. Turn a page and you send currents of air rippling through the room. Open the front door and a curtain will flap at the back of the house. Breathe and you inhale air breathed by others before. Move and it moves with you, stand still and it moves around you. The breeze you felt on your skin may be the tail end of a storm in Siberia or the beginning of a hurricane somewhere else.

Because it is agile, volatile, ever changing it is allied to the soul. The soul is moved by sympathy and antipathy as the air by warmth and cold. A faint feeling can in time, and sometimes in no time, turn into an emotional storm. And, surprisingly, an emotional storm can be calmed by a change in external weather.

All but our most determined thoughts are carried aloft of our inner moods as birds on currents of air; even our musings, deeper in winter and wider in summer, migrate with the seasons as swallows and geese.

All this bears witness to the tight relationship that exists between the inner and outer worlds; and it is the re-establishment of these relationships that a good part of poetry is about.

Exercise 4 Air

Time to air your pen. Remember to write with the element, rather than just about it. Let your writing breathe. Work your wings.

> *I have been a conch shell, taken from the niche in the hut's wall and tasted by the tribal elder, softened by his spittle as he tastes my saltiness and blown. Air rushing through my spiralled caverns, racing and rolling the porous walls, sluicing over the shining inner sanctum of my forgotten gut as it furiously ignites a sound of pain, a wrenching of command, a syllable of hope. Breath, and need, calling, crying, begging, beckoning, boasting, bellowing. He takes another deep, deep breath and from his bowels, his solar plexus, raging and expanding through his lungs and engorging his throat comes the urge, the furious need to call his tribe together.*
>
> *But only as it echoes through my chambers, only as I refine his wish, only as my boney, calcified form welcomes his pulsating, raging breath, only as my spiralling circuitous tracts marry with his impassioned need, only then does the echoing, baleful call ricochet through the hearts of the cowering tribe.*
> **Dale Irving**

Fire

Fire is the omnipresent king that penetrates all other elements. Burn a log and everything solid will turn to ash. While water and air will escape as smoke, fire will unfasten itself from matter as radiant warmth. It is the presence of fire that makes water into water, ice, or windswept cloud. It is the wheel of warmth that pushes the wind that pushes the ocean currents. The same wheel turns seawater into clouds and clouds into rain and rain into the solvent that returns everything solid back to the boiling bowels of the earth. And there, in the dense fire of her own forge, the earth fashions her own shape, making continents drift and mountains rise.

Fire in various forms turns sour grapes into sweet grapes, sweet grapes into wine, wine into brandy and brandy into flammable spirits. Subtler forms of the same fire ripen our decisions, ferment our turbid musings, and distil essential ideas from diffuse beginnings.

Inner fire is to the mind what warmth is to the world. We engage it in every creative act. Even in reading a poem. Only by means of this fire is static print brought into flow, flow lifted to feeling, and feeling fired by an understanding that matches the writer's initial intent.

In writing a poem we do the reverse. We start with the initial, fire-related intent, engage with feeling, and condense it to the flow of language until eventually it solidifies on the page. And there the poem will remain, waiting for a reader to strike new meaning from the rigidity of print.

Exercise 5 Fire

Now write a piece 'about' fire, inviting its nature into your writing. Engage your imagination if you want your readers to catch fire.

An Open Fire
Flame uncontained, frick thinly flick
mouth much slight searing
reap, reap with rising roar the ish of air
unriddle the crink and kite of lint
unravel the spit of spite,
the leap of heath hitched to night
preen pine, croon cross-eyed and switch tongues
to spin skint and hoar high the light imprint.
Jennifer Kornberger

Yes, I have been a dragon breathing fire. Finding breath to force my deep radiance out. I have this power-pit in my belly, this urge and force that rises and breaks and would burst through my scales devouring, roasting, consuming my form. I have summoned my breath, trained my will and forced that raging fire to blast from my fangs in a piercing barb that spears its prey and holds mortals hostage. I have been the potency of this sun-surge that brings villagers to their knees and knights to their sword. I breathe fire and dream of ice.
Dale Irving

Transformations

The elements are a kind of alphabet that can help us read (and therefore write about) the relation between inner and outer realities. Ice can change into water as stuck feelings melt into more fluid emotions. A sun-baked desert can evoke feelings of exhaustion or forbearance. Writers frequently use external surroundings to illustrate inner states or project inner states into external surroundings. *Coleridge's Kublai Khan,* for instance, maps an entirely inner landscape while *Wordsworth's Tintern Abbey* uses a real landscape to mirror the poet's soul.

In his poem *Fern Hill, Dylan Thomas*, Welsh bard and heir apparent to Taliesin's word-craft, remembers a childhood morning on a farm. The morning he describes speaks for the essence of childhood, of everything young, untainted, fresh. His experience evokes memories of paradise lost and, in a moment of poetic grace, temporarily regained. Inner and outer merge and the world is made whole again:

> And then to awake, and the farm, like a wanderer white
> With the dew, come back, the cock on his shoulder: it was all
> Shining, it was Adam and maiden,
> The sky gathered again
> And the sun grew round that very day.
> So it must have been after the birth of the simple light
> In the first, spinning place, the spellbound horses walking warm
> Out of the whinnying green stable
> On to the fields of praise.

In the next exercise we will attempt such wholeness by merging inner and outer realities.

Exercise 6 Inside out, outside in

There are two possible approaches to this exercise. You could begin with an external event, a landscape or scene in nature and allow it to speak for your inner world. Or you could begin with your inner world and transform it into an external event such as a landscape, scene or process in nature. You may find that in the act of writing, no matter where you start, inner and outer coincide.

> I have been the mountain. I have been in this place, upon this land, I have been this land since time began. I stand strong. I stand strong in the storms that rage and ravage, the winds that whip and worry and winnow and whirl. The breezes that whisper and waft through my plateaued meadows. The wind that scours the rock face, that lifts up and tosses the gravel

and the scree singing into the valley below.

I have been the mountain. I have been in this place, upon this land, I have been this land since time began. I stand strong. I stand strong in the driving rain that drums and drenches, soaks and scars. The rain that falls and flows upon my face, furrowing my stone into rushing stream and river wide. The rain that falls and flows into the mudslide and avalanche, that crumbles and crashes and crushes, with deafening boulder pounding, bouncing, gashing and thundering. The rain that falls and flows and steady pours, soft and silky polishing. The rain that forms in cloud and mist and fine drifting rainbow spatter making my stones jewel bright.

I have been the mountain. I have been in this place, upon this land, I have been this land since time began. I stand strong. I stand strong unassailed by the lightning strikes that cleave and crack. The wild fires that burn fierce and consuming down my flanks, that blacken and char and ashen carpet me. I stand strong in the noon day sun that bleaches the grasses and bracken, desiccating them into dust. I absorb the warmth into my bony depths, to ignite the molten core of me.

Samantha Bullock

DAY FOUR

Let us recall the story so far.

Ceridwen brews the cauldron of inspiration for her son Morfred. Gwion drinks of it instead and so gains the wisdom intended for Morfred and the gifts of a master bard. He flees from his mistress's anger. Pursued by her he becomes a hare, a salmon, a raven and much else. In the end he hides as a grain of wheat and is eaten by Ceridwen who has turned herself into a speckled hen.

But rather than this being his end it is the beginning of a new life. Ceridwen becomes pregnant and Gwion becomes her son. When he is born he is saved by his mother, put in a leather bag and set adrift on the sea. After three days he is found by the young prince Elphin.

Elphin was a luckless lad until he hauled in Taliesin. Sent to catch salmon, he had failed to net even one. Rueing his peculiar catch he cannot see that his fortune has turned.

Beginners in the poetic trade often resemble Elphin. They may find themselves gifted with an infant ability they had not looked for. It is a calling that can be heard or ignored, dismissed or followed. The danger of treating their 'catch' as irrelevant (or even as a misfortune) is great. The reason for this is usually self-doubt.

Self-doubt

Doubt is the immediate reaction to any form of calling, poetic or otherwise. Typically, this reaction is caused by an inability to express oneself, i.e. a lack of poetic or creative confidence.

Elphin's calling comes in the form of Taliesin. And it comes at a moment when his misfortunes have peaked. He has failed to make a catch when success was certain. To top it all he has ruined the good fortunes of the weir, disappointed his father, and exposed his incurable misfortune to the whole court.

Poetry often comes in times of crisis and moments of gloom. It is found in poverty, in prisons, in refugee camps, in situations of personal and collective despair.

Dante's Divine Comedy begins in just such a moment:

In the middle of my life
I suddenly awoke
Found myself in a wood so dark
That the road was wholly lost.

So cruel and lightless was this wood.
That I can hardly speak of it,
Mere memory stirs
Such terror in my blood,
That even now I feel
I am about to die.

Elphin is in such a situation. And today, with our faith in the future failing and the earth in distress; with depression epidemic, this is the situation that humanity is in.

A certain measure of misfortune is often needed to bring about change. Elphin, like Dante, needed a rock bottom experience to propel him upward again. In such situations the presence of a mentor is needed: for Dante this was Vergil, for Elphin it was Taliesin, who helped him with a song:

Fair Elphin, do not lament your fate
No catch at Gwyddo's weir
Was ever as good as today.

Dry your cheeks fair Elphin
For nothing is gained by sorrows.
Although you think yourself cheated
Your gain will be greater than your loss,
Though I am small
I am large in ability,
Though I am helpless now
I will bring help in time.

Fair Elphin, of generous mind,
Do not grieve any more
Though I was spumed
by Dylan's wave
I shall profit you more
Than all the salmon ever caught
At your father's weir.

Though I lie tied in a basket
There are wonders on my tongue,
And harm shall avoid you
When I am at your side.

Taliesin tells Elphin that whoever finds poetry finds luck. And the only real and lasting luck for poets is to be active, creative and connected with something more than themselves. To feel the flow of words, phrases and sentences, to partake in the creation of a piece of poetry or prose is an experience of transcendence that assures the writer of being embedded in a greater, more encompassing, more lasting and more meaningful self. It is as Wordsworth put it, an 'intimation of immortality,' an *anti-death dose* by means of artistic experience; a first, tender and yet utterly real crossing of a threshold into something greater than ourselves.

While poetry affords many pleasures to the reader, the crossover into a more creative self is reserved for the writer alone. The young bard's assurance that he will always be at Elphin's side is given to every poet: it is the promise of a muse, of a steady, unwavering companion in creative pursuits.

Though this promise is always given, it is not always heard. The moments of doubt make it particularly hard to hear. In such moments the help of the creative Taliesin-self is crucial. If the encouragement is missed or is not heard, progress is doubtful.

The next exercise will help this hearing.

Exercise 1 Taliesin's consolation

If you are a confident writer let your poet-self speak to your ordinary self in the way Taliesin spoke to Elphin. Let it tell you of the good fortune you already have simply by having a poetic self. Treat this self as an entity of its own; listen to it and prepare to be surprised by what you hear.

If you are a beginner (or a seasoned writer looking for a new spring) I suggest you do this exercise for someone other than yourself. Start by creating a clear image of this person in your mind's eye. See them walk and talk. Hear them speak. Notice the timbre of their voice, the way they wear their clothes, make their movements, conduct their affairs, how they write and read their poetry. Add as much detail as you can and then launch straight into the exercise.

You could even go a step further and allow your memory image to fade until only a feeling impression remains and then allow this impression to prompt you with your first line, a mood or soundscape that carries creative momentum or an image that may directly or indirectly inspire your work.

Muse

I am air, wind and fire
turn your stale breath
with the spin of words
turn your wordly tongue
to tongues of hope
casting your fingers
into pens of steel
claim a truth you doubt to see

I am perilous force
will turned courage
longing turned desire
filled with words that connect
generations and continents
rivers and mountains
forests of grief, love and belonging

I am the one that outlives your limited body
I am the gun that fires love
I am love that knows
no drought, no poverty, no prison
no stranded self

I am you
more than you
the best you
the un-you
the me-you
Tineke Van der Eecken

I Taliesin anoint you
with perfumed oil
deem you poet

I Taliesin breathe my
breath into your being
set on fire your
inspiration

I Taliesin place into your hands
the clay of words

I Taliesin gift you
the palette
of all feelings

I Taliesin give you
the intimacy of details

I Taliesin offer you
the broken pot
its shards quicken
what is hidden
births unknown
blossoms
Annette Mullumby

The Profits of Poetry

It is one thing to deal with your own doubt. It is another to deal with the doubt that others have about you and your poetic capacities.

Elphin is given hope by Taliesin's song and returns with newfound confidence. The court is assembled and hopes are high. His father is pleased to see him in high spirits and calls out: How many salmon have you caught today? And Elphin, assured by Taliesin's song, replies, 'I have got something better than salmon! I have caught a poet!'

The courtiers' cheer dies away. 'A poet? What will a poet profit you?' is Gwyddo's response.

Gwyddo's question is archetypal. It is often asked, though rarely aloud. Poetry is thought to be unprofitable. A painter produces something that can be sold. A journalist is capable of securing a job. A novelist has some chance of making a living. But there is little or no money to be made from poetry. It makes little commercial sense and hence no sense to those who measure their life against their bank balance.

But before Elphin can reply, Taliesin answers in his stead.

I will profit him more
than all the salmon ever caught
at Gwyddo's weir have ever profited thee.

Taliesin must answer if the argument is to be to be won. Elphin's arguments are as yet no match for those of his father. There is still too much conventionality in him to deal with others.

Taliesin's reply states the incomprehensible in conventional terms and the obvious by poetic standards. It literally reverses the established order of things by emphasising poetic engagement as the foremost of human tasks.

Exercise 2 The usefulness of poetry

Now it is your turn to defend your art. Imagine yourself speaking to someone who has an open or tacit disregard for poetry. Or even better, let your Taliesin-like self do the speaking for you.

You cast into the river and haul fish.
My nets spill stars onto the dark deck of your heart.

You send out your hounds of logic.
The quicksilver fox dozes by my fire.

When you lie in childbed, marriage bed,
deathbed your counterfeits dissolve and
you remember me.

I provide a hand, a boat, a lantern.
Liana Joy Christensen

Challenged in his conviction the king replies: '*Art though so small
a babe and so great a speaker?*'

This is not just the typical put-down the old occasionally inflict upon the young. Gwyddo's doubt in the authority of someone so small, so childlike, someone without reference, title or known lineage betrays the age-old conflict between poetry and establishment, creativity and convention.

Poetry, and particularly modern poetry, aspires to originality. The opposite of originality is conventionality, which in the realm of language surfaces as cliché. Good poetry today has no precedent, it is word by word innovation that results in unconventional language conveying unconventional thought. This can be challenging to those who think along the road most travelled (which is most of us most of the time).

Today this conflict is heightened by the general unease of our intellectual age with anything to do with poetry and imagination. In his book, *The Hatred of Poetry, Ben Lerner* illustrates this unease in a meeting between a poet and a dentist.

*There is an embarrassment for the poet – couldn't you get a
real job and leave your childish ways behind you? – but there
is also embarrassment on the part of the non-poet, because
having to acknowledge one's total alienation from poetry
chafes against the early association of poem and self. The
ghost of that romantic conjunction that makes the falling
away from poetry a falling away from the pure potentiality
of being human ...*

Of course, nobody objects to a little bit of poetry kept safely between the covers of books and put neatly on the shelf. Most people will appreciate a well-crafted line at a wedding or funeral. Even the occasional quote is welcome.

But a poet in person is another matter, particularly if that person is close. Suddenly there is another side to a wife, a new depth to a son. Family members may not always feel friendly towards that newcomer and friends and colleagues may feel just as challenged as the dentist in Lerner's book. In fact the poet too may be challenged by the pronouncements of a new-found self, a self that does not conform to pet opinions and habits of thought. Its originality demands radical changes.

Elphin suffers such a revolution of mind when Taliesin (his new-found poetic self) instructs him to view his greatest misfortune as his greatest luck. He is of course ready for this, as are many poets who experience a similar turn of events. Their family, friends, colleagues may not be so ready. Like Gwyddo they may need time to adjust. And they may, if only tacitly, defend themselves like Gwyddo, belittling the authority of the newly emerged poet.

Taliesin is not silenced by convention, authority, age or position. The child poet is quick to reply. And his reply is neither polite nor politic.

I can speak better
Than thou canst hear,
Give more answers
Than thou hast questions to ask.

The bard puts the king in his place, kicks away his pedestal and asserts the poet's right to chastise authority.

All poets must do this to their interior Gwyddo if their poetic self is not to be silenced. And at times they must stand up to those around them who express open or tacit disregard in a similar way. You can start doing it right now.

Exercise 3 The Poet confronts Gwyddo

Picture a particular relative, friend or colleague who might respond like Elphin's father. Don't speak to them yourself, but let your poetic self do the speaking for you. Let there be no doubt where your alliance lies. Don't be 'nice'. Be decisive, authoritative and original in your statements. Think of it not as a putting down, but a putting in place, an act of civil therapy. Here are two examples:

Gwyddo
You see up to a certain point,
Caged in opaque walls,
A dog chasing its tail.
The wind is foreign to you,
the sky clouded by heavy grey.
The stars wallow behind an electric sheath.

Can you not see beyond the plastic toys of your office?
Rubbery keys of your digital guide
Swirling, spinning, rocking.

A wanderer,
Listen.
Look at what has always been before you.
White glistening gems,
Hear the words before speech,
Evoked in nature's realism.
Tobias Robertson

Suck what marrow remains
in the broken bones
of your culture
the hunger will not abate
chitter and scrabble through
the towering heaps of e-waste

blue flames flicker
your eyes dart this way
and that
the light never lasts

Know this

I keep my campfire at the crossroads.
A small iron cauldron
swings above the flames.
It contains all you long for —
and cannot know.

You will be offered a small bowl.
It will sustain.
Liana Joy Christensen

Poetic Confidence

Nobody, of course, likes to be put in their place less than those in authority. When Gwyddo retorts: 'What or who are you?' he is saying: By what authority do you make such claims? What gives you the right to speak to me like this?

Taliesin immediately answers this challenge by asserting an authority beyond the ken of kings.

From the waters I came
With blessings great.

I am thrice born
And know by meditation
What was and will be.

I am versed in all sciences
I can read the ciphers of the stars.

I know the voices of the wind,
And the true names of trees.

I understand the tongue of the river
And the seven languages of the sea.

At first sight this claim may seem unfounded, even boastful. But it is consistent with convictions that older societies held about poets. In his introduction to *Lyrical Ballads, William Wordsworth* alludes to some of these. (While he refers to men only, it should go without saying that the passage is equally applicable to women.)

Who is a poet?

He is a man speaking to men: a man, it is true, endowed with more lively sensibility, more enthusiasm and tenderness, who has a greater knowledge of human nature, and a more comprehensive soul, than are supposed to be common among mankind; a man pleased with his own passions and volitions, and who rejoices more than other men in the spirit of life that is in him; delighting to contemplate similar volitions and passions as manifested in the goings-on of the Universe, and habitually impelled to create them where he does not find them. To these qualities he has added a disposition to be affected more than other men by absent things as if they were present.

To be affected by absent things as if they were present is the trait of the imagination and a prerequisite for empathy.

Imagine you hear in passing of an earthquake in Mexico. If you have no connection to anyone there the news may not affect you very much. But if you pick up a newspaper that features a picture of the devastation you may not remain untouched. Seeing parents desperately searching through the rubble for their children while watching the news may move you even more.

Now imagine that you do not see this picture on a screen but that you produce it vividly in your mind's eye. If you imagine it with great detail, if you see, hear, sense, smell, and taste the terror and despair of those involved you will inevitably be moved to compassion; you will start to feel the pain that earlier hardly touched you.

You will have become '*a more comprehensive soul, endowed with more sensibility, and tenderness*' – a more poetic human being no matter whether this incident stirs you to write or not. The imagination allows you to expand and empathise, to inhabit (or at least begin to inhabit) a space greater than yourself.

Imagination and empathy, are of course, in no way limited to human affairs. They can be applied to an endangered species, a wetland, a river, a forest or even a single tree. Nor are they restricted to things under threat. Our capacity to see, sense and participate in more than ourselves, to feel lifted by the swoop of a seagull, straightened by the steep rise of karri trunks and reassured by a slant of sunlight on the kitchen sink is intimately linked to it; so is our ability to be moved by a simple song or a Bach cantata, a Greek temple, a Rembrandt self-portrait, an essay by Emerson, an installation by Joseph Beuys or Marina Abramovich.

Exercise 4 Poets about themselves

Now you can trust your own Taliesin to confidently announce his or her poetic gifts. Remember you are not talking about yourself. It is the emerging Taliesin in you that gives account of him or herself.

I learned from the wind to open my lungs.
I can balance like a waterbird.
I have learned from the hedgerows the subtlety of weeds.
I have learned from the Taj Mahal the price of love.

From the Eiffel Tower, the reach of anticipation.

From the roar of the bush fire, the power of pursuing a questionable goal.

I have learned from the incessant television noise filtering through my open, summer window, the forbearance of strata living.

I have learned from the waves, the breath of mystery of the ebb and flow of life.

I have learned from the hot bitumen road the need to pause before running barefoot through the world.

Dale Irving

DAY FIVE

Elphin's luck did indeed change from the moment he met Taliesin.

Whenever there were questions, Taliesin knew the answer. When there was need, Taliesin found help. When there was conflict Taliesin helped with counsel. When there was sorrow Taliesin knew how to comfort.

When his father dies Elphin becomes king. And with Taliesin at his side he and his kingdom prosper.

Everything goes well until Elphin is called to appear at the court of the high king, his uncle Maelgwyn, famed for his bad temper and pride, and surrounded by sycophant courtiers and false bards, employed to sing unfounded praises rather than reveal relevant truths.

Elphin travels unwillingly, but it is his duty to attend. He is cautious, holds back and listens for a long time to the lavish praise heaped upon the king. But when the courtiers pronounce Maelgwyn's queen to be the most virtuous lady in the land, and when they hail the high king's bards as by far the best, he speaks his truth. This is soon related to the king. Challenged in his pride, Maelgwyn promptly puts his nephew under lock and chain, and sends his lecherous son Rhun to bring disgrace upon Elphin's queen.

Taliesin, by means of his art, already knows what is afoot and advises his foster mother to change apparel with the kitchen maid. Rhun is fooled, makes merry with the maid and puts her to sleep with a potion. In the morning he leaves with the right ring on the wrong finger.

Maelgwyn is delighted when Rhun returns with a token of success, but Elphin quickly proves the innocence of his queen. Maelgwyn however is not willing to let his nephew go until Elphin proves the superiority of his bard. Elphin sends messengers, but long before they arrive, Taliesin is already on his way. Before he leaves, he resolves to confront Maelgwyn's bards, and foresees the dire end of Maelgwyn and his court:

> *...Their lives shall be short*
> *And their lands laid to waste.*

To appreciate Taliesin's fierce reaction towards his fellow poets we must first understand the function of the ancient bards. They were the radio, television, movie, newspaper, and social media of their time. As the mouthpiece of their king, they were a mix of advertising agency and public relations team, employed to celebrate, promote, uphold, remember, praise, make sense, inspire and persuade. The songs they composed were repeated at every feast, and the phrases they coined made it to every ear. The king was omnipresent through their work.

Nothing much has changed. Modern politicians employ public relations teams and eloquent speech writers aided by journalists, reporters, bloggers and tweeters to transmit their message. In times of manufactured consent, when 'kings' are made by media campaigns much depends on contemporary bards, their way of handling their profession, their habits of using or abusing the word. The topic has lost none of its relevance.

Maelgwyn's bards, more keen to please the king than call him to account, have corrupted their calling and therefore the whole court. Everyone has been enjoined to proffer false adulation. Everyone except Elphin, whose association with Taliesin has made him sensitive to duplicity.

A moment comes when holding back his own opinion would make Elphin complicit with the public lies propagated by Maelgwyn's bards, and so Elphin speaks up.

This is what poets (and those who think like poets) have often done: Allied to their uncompromising art they have spoken up for the oppressed and rallied against injustice. They have written against the grain of public opinion, framed the difficult truth, and exposed easy lies. Putting pen to paper and paper to public opinion, they have roused masses from their trance, inspired change and sparked revolutions. Hence the proverbial notion of 'the pen is more powerful than the sword.' The dedication to inconvenient truth and unpopular insights invariably sets poets in opposition to those who abuse and manipulate the word.

The poet's task is authenticity, the kind of rare truth in which inner and outer, form and content, coincide. As the diaphanous art of revelation, poetry is opposed to any form of manipulation, deception, hidden or open lie. The poet *Jorie Graham* observes,

> *Each poem is in the end an act of mind that tries, via precision of seeing, feeling and thinking, to clean the language of its current lies, to make it capable of connecting us to the world.*

The aim of poetry is the truth and more than the truth. Not just what is true, but how it is true. The 'what' can after all be said prosaically. The 'how' requires poetry: the precise choice of words, the clear formulation and appropriate form. In poetry what is said is married to what cannot be said. It is expressed through the subtleties of tone, the in-between of lines, the mastery of form and composition. Poets purvey their truth by fusing feeling and thought, and by being so unreservedly themselves that they inspire others to do the same.

It is because of the poet's infectious authenticity and deep commitment to truth that they were called into the company of kings to assist them with advice. (The occasional presence of poets at the inauguration of American presidents is a remnant of this custom.)

Poetry is politic because the truth is politic and the ultimate standard of rule.

Coleridge's poem *Fears in Solitude* was written in April 1798, under the threat of a French invasion. Though concerned about the danger, Coleridge was not tempted to blame the enemy alone:

> *...We have offended, Oh ! my countrymen !*
> *We have offended very grievously,*
> *And been most tyrannous. From east to west*
> *A groan of accusation pierces Heaven !*
> *The wretched plead against us ; multitudes*
> *Countless and vehement, the sons of God,*
> *Our brethren ! Like a cloud that travels on,*
> *Steamed up from Cairo's swamps of pestilence,*
> *Even so, my countrymen ! have we gone forth*
> *And borne to distant tribes slavery and pangs,*
> *And, deadlier far, our vices, whose deep taint*
> *With slow perdition murders the whole man,*
> *His body and his soul ! Meanwhile, at home,*
> *All individual dignity and power*
> *Engulfed in Courts, Committees, Institutions,*
> *Associations and Societies,*
> *A vain, speech-mouthing, speech-reporting Guild,*
> *One Benefit-Club for mutual flattery,*
> *We have drunk up, demure as at a grace,*
> *Pollutions from the brimming cup of wealth ;*
> *Contemptuous of all honourable rule,*

Yet bartering freedom and the poor man's life
For gold, as at a market !

Coleridge delivers this testament of self-knowledge to his countrymen because he felt it was his poetic duty. He was enough of a Taliesin not to pander to what was convenient, fashionable and politically correct.

Coleridge and all poets who act like him are inevitably enraged by the dishonest manipulation of language. They are compelled to confront false bards wherever they meet them, knowing they confront the spurious in themselves too. All poets have to contend with their own false bards of personal habit and collective cliché, national and cultural prejudice and self-serving righteousness that obstructs poetic progress.

The next exercise will help you distance yourself from unwanted personalities and deluded phrasemakers, be they part of your own personal entourage or of the courts of this world. Taliesin's song applies to both.

I will go on my journey
Until I come to the gate
Of Maelgwyn, the king.
I will enter his hall
And silence the bards

I will humble the proud,
Undo the poets
Who ply their craft
For wicked ends,
The singers of false songs
And makers of evil schemes.

I Taliesin, chief of the bards
Will free fair Elphin
From his silver chains,

I will revenge my master
On Maelgwyn the High King
And his lecherous son,
Their lives shall be short
And their lands laid to waste.

Exercise 1 Taliesin's resolve

Let us take our lead from Taliesin's uncompromising stance and state our own resolve to confront false bards. Note the decisive 'I will' in all three stanzas: *I will go on my journey ... I will humble the proud and ... I will free Elphin ...*

You could start your writing in a similar way or find other entry points to say what needs to be said.

Resolve to Confront False Bards

Your words drip like treacle across my ears.
Once they may have rung like bells.
But now, dull glug that glues my eyes,
Fills my nose,
Drips across my lips,
Stains my teeth with its fallacy,
Falls to my chest and dribbles,
Like glaciers to my feet.

Only ants find succour in you.
My humanity abhors those sweet licks,
I no longer have my armour to reflect your insipid flow,
My skin and flesh now my certain cloth,
No burnished plate to conceal me in your reflection,
I repel your glutinous passage,

I find no thing in your sweet poison,
I am whole without you.
Peter Gemell

Today's demon
This isn't some fancy demon
Not impressive with fire and heft
And thunderous cries of battle

No, this is a creeping silent fungal infection

A slow growing darkness
That spreads persistently in damp corners
Awkward little unreachable places

Not obnoxious enough to have the people
Running into the streets

More of a low grade chronic illness
We learn to live with

A touch of suffocation
We chat about over coffee
Breeda McKibbin

Mumbling Spells

Taliesin arrives long before he is expected, and at a most opportune moment. The king has ordered a great feast and the bards are getting ready to sing his praises. Taliesin passes the guards, enters the hall, and makes himself inconspicuous in a corner. The king and his bards arrive. As they pass him Taliesin works his spell-craft and binds their tongues. When they open their mouths they can only mumble.

Have you ever been under a mumbling spell? I have. And more than once. Usually I only notice it after the fact, when I edit my work. Then I realise that much of what I put on the page was nothing but mumbling. I suddenly see the empty phrases, the fill in, the convenient formulation, the forced ending I had contrived to get on with the work. I succumbed to mumbling, I have been Heinin Vard who made it easy for himself.

And because I have experienced the mumbling in myself I can experience it elsewhere. Like most poets I can hear it in glib chat, commercial advertising and political propaganda, can detect it in the insatiable hunger of the press for sensational stories and in radio talk wearing words to stumps. I hear it when phrases are threshed from the husk of words, clichés repeated ad nauseam, when speakers fit their tongues to the contours of a lie. To the Taliesin in us, who watches unobserved from the corner of uncompromising truth, all this is nothing but mumbling.

Poets always suffer when the word is abused. But through such suffering they gain the courage to appear before the courts of this world and defend their calling. And it is through their dedicated work that shallow truths reveal their lack of substance, that lies are stripped to the bare bone of facts, and that illusions collapse.

The Lives of a Poet

Maelgwyn is enraged by the failure of his bards. Eventually, his master bard Heinin Vard manages to gesture toward Taliesin as the cause of the mumbling. The king has Taliesin brought before him and questions him as to why he has vexed the bards.

Taliesin replies by stating who he is, for who he is explains what he does:

I am Taliesin,
Chief bard I am to Elphin
And the summer stars are my home,
Once I was called Merlin
But now I am known as Taliesin.

I was in the heavens
When Lucifer fell to the depths,
I bore the banner before Alexander
I know the stars in North and South
I was in Canaan when Absalom was slain
I was in the court of Don before the birth of Gwdion
I have been a year and a day in the fortress of Arianrod

I was loquacious before I was gifted with speech
I witnessed the destruction of Sodom and Gomorrah
I was the architect of Nimrod's tower
I was in India before the building of Rome
I upheld Moses in the waters of Egypt,
I have been under the cross with Mary Magdalen,
I have received the Muse from Ceridwen's cauldron,
I have been bard to Lleon of Lochlin
I have been on the White Hill at the court of Cynvelyn,

I have been fostered in the lands of the deity,
I have taught all ages and instructed all spheres,
I shall remain until the last day of the world.
No one knows if my body is flesh or fish.

For nine months I was in the womb of Ceridwen,
Once I went by the name of Gwion
But now I have become Taliesin.

This too is typical for poets. They reveal themselves in their work. A work of poetry is saturated with the poet's life: childhood, tears, struggles, victories and defeats, love and loves lost, travels, interests, inclinations, their whole complicated, involved, riddled existence. Not that a poet's work is always autobiographical; often it is not. But even then, and perhaps especially then, we meet a poet more intimately in one stanza describing dust motes than we meet a journalist relating, say, a personal experience in a recent war. Poets are what they write. They write what they are. Every line is a piece of life, every poem a biography. And more than one biography, for poets live multiple lives. By means of imagination their own life extends into that of others, and the present age into the ages that preceded it.

History is the poet's extended biography. But poets are not historians, they are 'storians' – concerned with essentials rather than accidentals. Already *Aristotle,* a great admirer of their art, realised that:

> *The difference between the historian and the poet is not that the one writes in prose and the other in verse. The difference is that one tells of what has happened and the other of the kinds of things that might happen. For this reason poetry is something more philosophical and more worthy of serious attention than history. For while poetry is concerned about universal truth, history treats of particular facts.*

Poets, in other words, relate to the story in history, to the universal meaning In the particular event. Through their imagination writers readily recognise themselves in Homer's epics, Dante's Commedia, Shakespeare's plays and Goethe's Faust, and in the great novels of recent times.

Poets are connected to these works even if they have not read them. They are 'familiar' because they were produced by their own kin, by forerunners who turned history into the biography of humanity. And to this biography poets have an intimate relationship. It is their own story.

It is by recalling this greater story that Taliesin justifies himself before Maelgwyn. In front of the whole court he remembers history as we remember our own life. History, not as the abstract accumulation of data and dates, but as the biography of the universally human.

Taliesin's claims obviously exceed what our ordinary memory is capable of. But what is beyond our memory is within reach of our imagination. Writers are not limited by their own story; every play and novel testifies to their ability to inhabit other lives. Using their imagination writers 'remember' what they have not experienced. Taliesin, the archetypal poet, claims all the memory of humanity as his own.

Now it is your turn to do the same. Being the apprentice rather than the master you will take a couple of steps where Taliesin took one stride, and start with a story you already know. Your own life. Here you can rely on memory and add imagination where memory fails.

Exercise 2 Memory list

Make a list of some of the important events that have shaped your life. Focus on essentials rather than externalities. Trust your memory and imagination and immediately write down what they provide you with. Refrain from judging the choice; long forgotten or seemingly irrelevant events may have meanings you cannot fathom.

> I was in Mary Gilmore's flat when she discussed writing with my father;
> I was at Gallipoli when my uncle climbed the cliffs and survived;
> I was on the streets of Perth when my Junior results were posted on the board outside the West Australian newspapers office.
> **Trisha Kotai-Ewers**

Exercise 3 The personal story

Now elaborate one of your personal memories. Take one of the lines you have written as a starting point and add as much detail as you can. Here are a few examples.

At South Hampton Pier the huge ship looms.
The little girl hugs tight the Panda her mother had made
The father puts down his battered suitcase
begins to tap-dance, as he hums 'Singing in the Rain'
The mother says 'Stop this nonsense, you are making an exhibition of yourself.'
The child props her Panda against the hatbox, grabs her father's hand.
He swings her up and onto his shoulders. She clutches his forehead and together they dance against the mother's blank back.
Annette Mullumby

My Father's Death
As the breath of the father left his body
His wife cradles his head in her arms as the breath of the father left his body;
The daughter falls onto her lover's shoulder as the father's breath left his body;
The grand-daughter, separate from the others,
puts her hand on the father's hand,
feels his hairs against her palm, as the father's breath left his body;
The brother's hand wipes his eyes, as the father's breath left his body;
The nurse peeps into the room, retreats, as the father's breath left his body;
The room falls into stillness, no-one moves,
as the father's breath left his body;
The daughter breaks the stillness,
puts her hand on the mother's shoulder;

The mother turns, takes the daughter into her arms,
as the father's breath left his body;
the daughter's lover touches
the arm of the grand-daughter.
The picture moves without sound
as new groupings form, new connections are made;
until the father lies alone in his bed,
the breath having left his body.
Trisha Kotai-Ewers

Exercise 4 Imaginary list

And now do what Taliesin did. Claim history as your story. List at least seven events you have witnessed or been part of. Use your imagination where Taliesin used his memory. There is no need to know history and don't worry about chronology. (Taliesin's is jumbled too).

Note that Taliesin was more a witness than an actor. He bore the banner before Alexander rather than being Alexander. Do likewise and avoid grandiose claims. It is much better to be to be the second kitchen maid of Napoleon's sister in law than Napoleon. It may help you to start with the line *I am Taliesin. I have been/ seen / witnessed/ ....*

I sat at the feet of Dante as he spoke of the inferno
I danced upon the stage as Pavlova dancing the Dying Swan;
I walked the streets of Rome in the days after Caesar's murder;
I heard Anthony give Caesar's eulogy;
I was in the audience at the first performance of Shakespeare's first play;
Trisha Kotai-Ewers

I was the arc in a wilderness of water
I was the flames that flailed London
I was the icebound body of a German soldier

I was the spittle in Hitler's throat
I was the seven lean cows that ate up the seven fat ones.
Annette Mullumby

Exercise 5 The trans-personal story

Now let us work with your imaginary memories. Choose one of your lines and launch straight into the narrative. If this is difficult, crank up your writing motor through a series of variations on the first line (as practised earlier on). Once you have gained momentum write on and into the topic of your tale.

Proceed as you would with your own memories: Start with one image and then see it through to the next. Practise moment to moment, image by image awareness. Trust the movie-maker in your mind's eye and you will find your imagination is ready to roll on its own accord. Impelled by pictorial logic and poetic evidence a greater Taliesin-like memory will inform yours.

Salt march
I heard the crunch-crunch
of sand and gravel
under his well worn sandals.

It started with two,
grew to four, twelve, seventy eight,
a hundred feet.

Slowly it swelled,
a train of men, kids and women,
sweating and marching
under the Indian sun.

Onlookers on the sidewalk
chattered, some critical,
some bemused,

others offering cow's milk or dhal,
small clusters joining the march
in twos and threes.

Onward he strode,
sun glistening
beads of sweat
rolling from his bald scalp
along the artery on his temple
and down his thin brown face.
His perfectly round spectacles
sliding down his nose,
poked back up to the bridge
by his left index finger.
His right hand holding a staff
swung out in front of him
to bite into the earth
with quiet determination ...
Hessom Razavi

Exercise 6 Trading lines

Now it is time to extend your poetic comfort zone. Ask a fellow
writer to give you a beginning line and elaborate on it in a piece of
writing. Remember that Taliesin remembers everything and trust
your imagination to lead you where you have never walked or
even thought of walking before. This will make your journey more
adventurous and your writing more alive.

If you work on your own choose one of the following options.

I have been a Polish housewife, peeling potatoes for eternity.
Tiffany Gee

I was at the inquisition of the Maid of Orleans.
Sally Davidson

I washed the dust from Cleopatra's skin
Karen Peradon

Here are two examples inspired by the same line:

I washed the dust from Cleopatra's skin

She lies there, lifeless. A calm serene smile. A small white cloth protects her modesty, even in her death she demands secrecy and respect. The sound of the room is made up of the echoes of movement; shuffling feet, the clanging of instruments. No one talks. We look and smile; raised eyebrows tell a thousand words. We know each other, the servants and I.

We hear each others thoughts like whispers on the wind. Oh! The things we have seen and dare not speak. I watch the sponge as I gently squeeze streams of water over her legs. It pools on the cloth below, creating coloured shapes, which outline her body.

Claire Williamson

I wash the dust from Cleopatra's body

She is cold, white, lifeless. She lies naked, half covered in shroud, raised on a high wooden table. Together with two other handmaidens I prepare her. Heavy gold in elaborate and decorative forms is placed on her forehead, around her neck, on her arms, around her wrists, on her feet, on her toes, around her ankles. I wash the dust from Cleopatra's body with a silk cloth. Her skin is of mysterious stone, almost translucent, green veined, opalescent, becoming statue.

Lyndsay Humphries

Poetic Errands

When Taliesin had finished singing of his many lives, Maelgwyn and his court marvelled greatly at what they had heard. The king ordered Heinin Vard to sing a reply, but all he could do was mumble. Realising that his bards were no match, the king asked Taliesin what his errand was and again he replied with a song.

I have come to measure myself
Against the king's bards,

To win back my lord Elphin
From the belly of the tower
And loosen the chains that hold him
Prisoner in this place.

Maelgwyn's question and Taliesin's reply are timely as our tasks inevitably grow from who we are and who we have been. Taliesin announces his mission – to liberate Elphin – immediately after revealing who he is and who he has been.

It is the same task poets have always undertaken by means of their art: the liberation of the ordinary self by the poetic self. From the perspective of the poetic self the ordinary self is always bound by its limitations, its outlook; it is imprisoned in a dungeon of its own making and chained by an intellectuality it cannot escape (the silver chains represent the reflective mind). Unless Maelgwyn and his bards are overcome, Elphin will remain in bondage.

Exercise 7 The errand

It is time to state your errand, or mission. Taliesin does this in the archetypal manner befitting a master bard. You have to be inventive if you want to do more than imitate him. To do this avoid generalisations, easy-come-concepts and clever conclusions. They arrest rather than liberate. Focus on your task as a poet, writer and creative human being. Write about where, how, who and what you are at this pen-point in your life. Weigh your current writing practice on the scales of your destiny and then draw the balance on the sheet before you. Be precise and honest.

I have come so that ears full of shrieks may hear the slide of
a snail on leaf
I have come so that the puppet of the body can dance to its
own string quartet
Annette Mullumby

Each word a seed. My task is to supply what is needed: smoke, fire, rain. When required, my sharpened nib scarifies the hard casing of cliché. Whatever germinates does not belong to me.

My work is a sabot hurled into the meaningless chatter of virtual circuitry. It seems urgent; it is not. Each age has its duties.

Released back to silence, I turn away and walk barefoot between night and day to the place where time is counted differently. Like poets of all the ages, I offer my work as a small wedge to prop open the door to eternity.

Liana Christensen

DAY SIX

Let us again start by recalling the story so far.

Gwion drank of the cauldron of inspiration and became the master bard Taliesin. As a babe he is hauled from the sea by the luckless Elphin. He tells Elphin that his luck will improve now that he is at his side. They return together and Taliesin successfully defends himself and his art before Elphin's father, Gwyddo, and the court.

Elphin's fortunes do indeed improve and after his father's death he becomes king. All is well until he is called to appear at the court of his proud uncle, the high-king Maelgwyn. When he speaks up against his uncle's unfounded claims he is put into prison. Maelgwyn and his son Rhun conspire to prove Elphin wrong, but fail to disgrace his queen. Taliesin is sent for and arrives long before expected. He binds the king's bards with a spell and sings of his greater memory.

After he states his errand Taliesin immediately launches his attack on the false bards.

> *If you were bards*
> *You would know the mysteries*
> *And declare them to the world.*
> *If you were bards*
> *You would know the terrible beast*
> *Rising from the abyss,*

The obnoxious creature
Who rules the shallows and the deep

If you were bards
You would know him
Whose jaws are wide as mountains
Whom neither weapons
Nor strength will subdue,
The one with the ice cold eye
In his head.

If you were bards
You would know
Falsehood from truth
And tell your king
Of the terrible creature
That will come from the sea-marsh
To devour him and his kin.

The tight staccato of events tells us that 'false bards' and 'true errand' are inversely related. Unless our errand clearly asserts itself against lesser objectives and illusory side-tracks, it is easily lost.

It is in life as it is on the page, where every piece of writing has a mission of its own, an errand to complete. The writer's task is to give way to a poem's unique intent and not be led astray. The struggle for the right word in the right place, the original line, the spirited formulation and the appropriate form cannot be neglected. It is a battle that must be fought daily and won daily.

Taliesin knows this struggle and attacks Maelgwyn's bards fiercely; his prediction is dire and the mood apocalyptic.

He invokes the sacred calling of the bard and accuses Maelgwyn's minstrels of having forsaken it. He charges them with blindness as to the effect of their work and foresees Maelgwyn's ruin as a result. He reveals the demonic, the inherently destructive side of their misuse of language. He points to the high level of responsibility attached to word-work, and the dire consequences when it is ignored. The master poet is alert to the real, deeper, moral causes of calamity. He knows that a monstrous attitude will have a monstrous effect. He is aware of the subtle interplay between attitude and weather, self and world, community and environment.

Exercise 1 Poetic Confrontations

Let us do the same. Speak directly to the false bards of your world, be they exterior or interior. Be strong, clear, bold, challenging. Say what needs to be said.

> *You rip the tongues of truth*
> *you scald eyes*
> *fill ears*
> *with molten lava*
> *drown the hunkered heart*
> *pull nails from fingertips*
> *collapse the voice box to a squeak.*
> **Annette Mullumby**

> **Black Flowers**
> *You have been a towering beast,*
> *Invoked by my mother and my mother's father,*
> *Feared by my father and my mother's mother.*
> *A hungry hairy obnoxious monster*
> *Sowing seeds of self-doubt*
> *Growing forests of strangler vines,*
> *Black flowers bearing teeth and wicked grins.*
> *Insidious whispers,*
> *Weakness, confusion, mind fog and anxiety,*
> *Frozen potential, stunted and gnarled.*
> *A graveyards of dreams.*
> **Tiffany Gee**

In spite of Taliesin's predictions Maelgwyn is unwilling to let

Elphin go. Seeing that his efforts are to no avail, Taliesin summons the wind by means of a song.

Know thou the strong one
From before the flood;
Without flesh, without bone,
Without vein, without blood,
Without hands, without feet
Who will not be older or younger
Than when he began.

The sea pales
When he approaches,
Great are his gusts
When he comes from the south,
White foam stirs
When he strikes from the coast.
Without hand, without foot
Without youth, without age
He was never born
And never grows old.
He Is us wide as the earth
He will not come when desired
Nor leave when asked
His course is unknown,
He is indispensable
He is without equal

He is four-sided;
He is unfettered
He is incomparable;
He will not be advised,
He commences his journey
Above the high rocks
He is sonorous, he is dumb,
He is mild, he is strong,
He is bold

When he glances over the land,
He is clamorous,
On the face of the earth.

He will destroy
But not repair the injury;
He is wet, he is dry,
He commences his course
From the heat of the sun,
And the cold of the moon.

Among all beings
One has prepared him
To wreak vengeance
On Maelgwyn, the King.

When he began singing a breeze began to stir. The breeze turned into a wind and the wind into a storm. Soon the storm raged so furiously that Maelgwyn thought the walls of his stronghold might break.

This story strikes an alarmingly familiar tone today when serious weather changes are shaking our world awake. The elements, it seems, have taken sides, and nature herself is storming against the ramparts of human hubris.

It seems as if Taliesin sings the storm into being, but he is no shallow magician using the elements to his advantage. He does not cause the storm. The storm comes because it is already there, already raging, already crashing against the king's hall. If it is man-made, it is made by Maelgwyn and his sycophant bards. Taliesin simply reveals what is.

Poets often do that. They are portals through which the hidden becomes manifest. Writers tend to reveal more readily, and more uncompromisingly, what will be because in fact it already is. With their art attuned to the subtleties of here and now, their pen becomes an antenna for things 'to come'. Poems surprise us with what we already know. The sort-of obvious becomes fully obvious when expressed well – at least to those who understand poetry and metaphor. Those who don't need further translation into the literal prose of reality.

Maelgwyn and his kind only learn by way of the stick that hits them, the storm that breaks their halls, the crisis they cannot escape. Today the environmental crisis is that stick. It is an obvious metaphor come to haunt us in the form of reality, a calamity caused by collective ignorance. And this ignorance is not due to any lack of knowledge, as it is largely because of our current knowledge that we have endangered the world.

Taliesin knew the world in other ways. He could 'call' the wind because he was familiar with the wind, knew its becoming, its approach, its ways, its worldwide working. He knew its particular manifestations, moods, will, and intent. He did not know it in the way we know today, by means of abstract reasoning and experiment. He knew the wind in the same way he knew the hare and the hound, the salmon and the fox, the sword blade and the cry in the midst of battle. He knew by knowing *with*, by identification, by being one with it. The Celtic bard still experienced the original, timeless entity of the wind, *the strong one from before the flood, who will not be older or younger than when he began.* He sang about the 'wind in all winds' who is simultaneously *sonorous and dumb, wet and dry, hot and cold.* But how do we, who live so solidly in the here and now, who are tied to tangible things and facts, approach such overarching realities?

Maybe by contemplating wind and weather, river and lake in new ways, in ways that do them more justice.

The River in all Rivers

To begin with we see a river the way we see everything else. As something out there and therefore separate, in the stasis of everything tainted with thought.

A river is in constant flow. Film it and it becomes flat. Photograph it and it becomes fixed. Think it and it becomes abstract. Observe and it comes closer. Recall it vividly and it comes to life. The river out there begins to flow in you. Intensify this experience and your mind overflows into the greater river, the river not seen, not thought, but imagined.

This greater river is its whole catchment, a web of tributaries narrowing into creeks, rivulets, trickles, wells and temporary springs; it comprises all moving water and all water patiently waiting in puddles, swamps, ponds and stagnant lakes; all the waters washed over granite and sucked into limestone, seeping through the gossamer of sand, soaking into the spongy earth, accumulating in underground aquifers, circulating through the arteries of rock.

This expansive river holds every drop that has run over tarmacs and trickled down rooftops, raincoats and cars, that has skimmed over boulders, wetted every rock, touched every grain of sand, that has dripped from rain-soaked trees and slid over every kind of leaf, stem and bark;

And this greater river is linked to the river system of plants: the myriad slow-motion rivulets rising from root to stem, the column of water slowly moving at the speed of growth, every leaf a slow-release estuary feeding moisture into the vertical river, the invisible spirals of humid air that rise above us like imperceptible trees whose canopies are the visible clouds.

This river beyond the river bed extends into everything wet, moist, fluid; it hovers in fogs, falls in drizzle, and condenses in dew. We are at all times surrounded by it: we walk inside this invisible river, sleep in its subtle eddies, are carried by currents we cannot see. The same ubiquitous river spouts from taps, gathers in pots, pools in kitchen sinks, steams in baths tubs, churns in washing machines and wears polar icecaps in freezers and fridges. It extends into our bodies, mingles with our blood, flows through arteries and veins, pools in our organs and keeps the brain buoyed inside our heads.

Inundated by this greater river our mind becomes more fluid, and our understanding pictorial and therefor poetic: the result is a beholding that is both thinking and seeing at the same time.

Exercise 2 Imaginative contemplation

Choose an elemental force such as wind, cloud, rain, sea, thunder or drought, or a landscape feature such as a desert or a lake. Then contemplate it in all its manifestations like Taliesin does. Start with what you see or know or remember and expand from there. Water it with your imagination. Hear the thunder in all its tonal variations, observe the sea in all its changes, variations, moods. Attempt the biography of a raindrop, the genesis of a thunderstorm, the forming and reforming of clouds.

If you find this exercise difficult, follow Taliesin's example and address an imaginary audience by using an entry phrase like *'Know thou the rain...'* or *'Consider the thunder...'*

Clouds
The frolic of fleecy white clouds, tinged with pearl
The repose of long streaks of fine cloud
Heavy, rolling thunder clouds, loud and heaving, trundling across the sky, darkening the land
Clouds on fire in the setting sun, full of drama and portent
Clouds, light hearted and blushing pink in the mornings
Clouds that are hurried
Clouds that are still
Clouds that bring welcome shadows on hot afternoons
Clouds that peep from their mothers' skirts
Layers of cloud, sharing the sky
Lonely little clouds in a wide expanse of blue
Jane Crothers

Dawn

Have you considered the emerging of colour as the light softly beams into day, the growing lushness of green vegetation, the burnished pindan earth. Have you considered the moment of subtle shift, of the awakening world to hope. Have you considered the light that warms from the night's chill. Have you considered the candle flame that opens the dark mystery?

The light in the window welcoming. The light of the stars remembering.

Have you considered the light of the epiphany of the new idea?

Have you considered the warming, hopeful creature that embraces the world, longitude by longitude, fondling the great planet in its generous, open palm, turning it slowly, moment by moment?

Dale Irving

Memories Immediate and Delayed

Now it is time to write about the river down the road, the clouds in sight, the rain that is falling right now, the lime-tree in front of you. You can do this either through direct experience in the present or by remembering such an experience at a later date.

In the first case observe what is before you in great detail and then write about what you have just seen, heard, sensed, and felt. The more attentive you are, the more fully you can immerse yourself in your surroundings, the more senses you involve, the more satisfying will be the result.

The second option starts in the same way, but reserves the act of writing for a later time. Wordsworth called this 'recollection in tranquillity.' Through sustained practice memories that appear faint at first can in time become uncannily intense. You may hear a long forgotten frog splash nearby, feel the cool breeze on your cheek, or see a black swan gliding inconspicuously in the shade of a boathouse. Sensations you hardly noticed can come to new and sometimes unsuspected life. And this life can lead to feelings that resonate deeply with the riverine world.

Here, or course, it is important to distinguish self-referential emotions from feelings that inform. If for instance, you dislike the water because you resented swimming lessons you are experiencing a self-referential emotion. Behind such emotions exists deeper, more receptive and highly resonant layers of feelings that can tell you how the brackish water lapping at your feet feels rather than how you feel about it. These layers subtly imitate whatever you see, hear, and experience. Becoming aware of layers means to be reddened in the presence of red, lifted into the flight of gulls, widened by the thin horizon skirting the sea, quickened by waters tumbling over granite boulders. The qualities of rock and river, weather and wind, lake and sea will begin to shape your writing. A slow flowing river will steady your rhythms, wet your page with watery consonants and pool the right vowels in the right places. A rugged mountain range will toughen up your prose, the size of a pond determine the length of your poem and the staccato of sedges inform the meter of your verse. Your language will become more artistic and onomatopoeia will occur of its own accord.

So will synaesthesia. You will begin to sense the colour of cold, hear the high pitch of yellow, see the sharp contours of precise thought. Awake to this layer you will start to experience the velvety texture of indigo skies and the soft touch of cobalt blue lining the horizon. Living into this 'language before words', you will start to sense the personality of the river, the individuality of the storm that stopped you in your tracks or the being of the landscape you live in.

Exercise 3 Mining Memories

No matter if you work with immediate experience or pictures drawn from the past you will need to recollect them in the act of writing. Do this using as much detail as possible. See and hear again what you have seen and heard. Excavate obvious and not so obvious experiences and become aware of the sensations accompanying them. What matters is that you shift from reactionary feelings to feelings that inform as you enter into a dialogue with more than yourself. Allow the cloudscape to shape your feeling and the river to pour through your pen.

The example below captures an experience with the Derbal Yerrigan or Swan River at Heathcote near Perth, Western Australia.

> ***The River - June Solstice***
> *The river, fat with sky*
> *waits for us to arrive;*
>
> *as we step*
> *out of the car*
> *it breathes out.*
>
> *A solitary plume of vapour*
> *hangs above the water*
> *close to the shore*
>
> *moulding and re-moulding*
> *a shape without sides*
> *turning the morning*
> *on its floating axis.*
>
> *The body of mist*
> *leans into space*

it opens to reveal
a swarm of droplets,
ecstatic in first flight;
they spiral up
scaling the light,

and we find the river
is standing before us

like a snake standing
on its tail

and we wait
on the shore
of the year

for the sky
to consume

its own skin.
Jennifer Kornberger

Identification

The next step is identification, becoming one with. The aim of identification is to know something the way you know yourselves. This requires a radical shift of perspective, a thorough transformation of the self into another by dint of will. And though this may be far beyond your scope, it is not beyond that of Taliesin, your poetic self. This self already knows the 'who' of the river, the numinous presence that makes the Wye into the Wye, and that distinguishes Danube from Don.

Exercise 4 Becoming one with

With this in mind continue with the same topic and stretch the poetic imagination to the point of identity. This means not just describing the river or bushland, but becoming it.

You can attempt this artistically by using the 'I am' form, giving river or cloud or wetland your voice. Doing this, the ordinary self may be stretched beyond its comfort zone, but the poetic self will be right at home for it has never left. It *is* the river and will gladly speak in its tongue. So rather than speak about the river, let the river, the beach, the open fire, speak through you. Give the wetland, piece of bush, patch of coast, your voice. Trust that your attempt will make the river, lake or pond incline toward you, become your muse, someone to write with rather than write about. Instead of being a lonely writer squeezing poetry from dried-up pen you might find yourself inundated with ideas.

I am the East wind
I pitch out of the desert
where the soil
is a skeleton
the night is reptile
and the stars
are the eyes
of animals
you've never seen.

I bring you easterly things
the lays of laterite
the authority of ironstone
the broken voice
of schist.

When I reach
the wheatbelt

I tighten one notch
gust through leaves
of gimlet gum;

I have chaff
and gold dust
in my mouth
strange pollens
on my breath

I come
to subdue
the sea
the juvenile coast.

Lay your table
in the open
and I'll serve
you crumbs
from the earth's
oldest crust.
Jennifer Kornberger

I am night;
I always was;
I always will be.
Possessor of worlds,
I take hold,
I let go.
I suspend the stars in my deep waters.
I am deeper than the sea
and darker.
I am the sea of the sky.
Kevin Mazzer

Exercise 5 The choice of lines

Now you have gone this far, you can go further. Allow one of your fellow writers to gift you a line. This will help you to identify with things that you may not have chosen, but that have, via your co-writers chosen you. If you work on your own, choose one of the following:

> I am the West wind
> I am dawn
> I am the next drought
> I am the salt of the Wheatbelt
> I am all grasses around the globe
> I am a mountain

Here an example exploring dawn:

> I am dawn.
> I sing the world into being
> I slip into night
> on a silver slipper,
> fading the fabric of the stars
> until the kookaburra
> heralds my coming.
> I creep quietly onto the dark stage
> and take my place
> behind the velvet curtains.
> I set the world ablush,
> as I gently lift night's skirt
> and sweep the sky
> of all the stars.
> **Anni Gemell**

I suggest you attempt the 'I am' exercise with topics such as elemental forces, substances, places, plants, beasts, even inanimate things. It pays to repeat the previous stages before attempting to become one with mountain or thunder or sea. It is the safest way of widening the self, of becoming, as Wordsworth put it, 'a more comprehensive soul, endowed with more sensibility and tenderness' towards the world.

Such Taliesin-like sensibility is much needed in an age that struggles to preserve rainforests, halt the pollution of oceans, arrest climate change and save the earth from calamity. It produces poetry not only on the page, but also in the world. This is, after all, what the story tells us. The Celtic bard turns the fortune of Elphin, secures his master's reign, confronts fake bards, chastises the court and exposes Maelgwyn's unmerited claims.

Most importantly he shows a sensitivity towards his environment that we have lost. He was still able to work with nature rather than against it, use the wind without abusing it. As a master poet he calls the storm because he is called to do so. And the storm comes and forces Maelgwyn to fetch his nephew from prison.

When Elphin was brought before the court, Taliesin loosened his chains with a charm. Then he sang another song in praise of all bards who stand by their calling.

The Excellence of Bards

What was the first man
Made by the gods;
What was his speech
What was his meat, what his drink,
What roof his shelter;
What his first sight
What the first thought

Of his thinking;
What the clothing;
That covered his form.

Wherefore should a stone be hard;
Why should a thorn be sharp-pointed?
Who is hard like a flint;
Who is salt like brine;
Who is sweet like honey;
Who rides on the gale;

Why is the nose straight;
Why is the wheel round;
Why is the tongue gifted with speech;

If thy bards, Heinin, be competent,
Let them reply to me, Taliesin.

The king's bards hung their heads and none dared reply. Thus the contest was won and Elphin freed. Right glad was Taliesin and right glad was Elphin, his master.

Taliesin wins his contest with a song composed of questions. He queries into the first and most important of all stories, the story of creation, the origin of the human being and the meaning of existence; he asks questions that can only be answered by a 'true' bard, by someone who like him

...grew learned in ancient laws
And in the speech before words...

Who, like the master bards of his tradition were

thrice born

and knew by meditation
was and will be....

By someone, in other words, who can tell of creation because he remembers creation. His questions are clearly a test that Maelgwyn's bards could not pass. But can we?

Questions and questions

There are questions that can be quickly answered because the knowledge is available.

Then there are deeper questions that take time. Such questions are answers in the state of becoming, incomplete intuitions that hover in the state of creative suspense until they are solved. Questions like this make us travel for a long time before we arrive. And they make sure we experience much before we get there.

Then there a third set of questions that omit arrival altogether as they cannot be answered. They live in the sphere of pure potentials. Such questions emphasise the journey, point to a quest. Depending on who hears them they mean everything or nothing.

A question like *Why is the wheel round?* lifts us straight to its level and resists all attempts to lower itself to ours. It is a kind of Celtic koan that invites us to come to where it came from.

And where it came from is the same place where poetry comes from. Writers enter and exit this place all the times. So does everybody who thinks new thoughts and constructive ideas. It is where our creative-self constantly lives and where our ordinary-self occasionally visits. It is where Taliesin permanently resides and where questions, like the ones he posed to Maelgwyn's bards, are continuously asked and answered in the act of writing.

Exercise 6 The quest for questions

With this in mind let us do what Taliesin did and ask questions that are simple but potent like his. Let us follow Pablo Neruda's advice:

> *...and I wrote the first faint line,*
> *faint, without substance, pure*
> *nonsense,*
> *pure wisdom of someone who knows nothing,...*

I suggest you try to be '*someone who knows nothing*' if you want to ask questions that mean everything, questions that can help you, as Neruda *put it, to see 'the heavens unfastened'*.

> *Where does morning go?*
> *What is the name of the night?*
> *Who kindles the sun?*
> **Ben Miller**

> *What was the first word?*
> *Who remembers how it tasted?*
> *Was it verb or noun?*
> *Did lips speak it?*
> *Or did it speak the lips?*
> *What tongue held the world, quivering, cupped?*
> **Genevieve Arden**

Here are some examples from a workshop in Bangalow, Byron Bay:

What is the light looking for?	**Tiffany Gee**
Why does water always level?	**Sally Davison**
Does a butterfly breathe?	**James Carlopio**
Why are black sheep black?	**Tobias Robertson**
Why does the sun?	**James Carlopio**
Can ideas think for themselves?	**Tobias Robertson**

Who became the seagull?	**Janet Paterson**
Where does grief go?	**Samantha Bullock**
What does life hear?	**James Carlopio**
Why can't we imagine another colour?	**Tobias Robertson**
Why does fire take so long?	**Sally Davison**
Why do we bother to ask questions, and	
not question ourselves for bothering?	**Tobias Robertson**

Take Taliesin's questions as a manual for poetic process. They tell us that we must become unknowing before we can know more thoroughly, speak naively to speak wise, risk complete innocence to reap experience that is poetic.

Whenever we lift ourselves to where such questions come from we apprentice ourselves to Ceredwin. We fire up the pot of potential, stir the cauldron of creativity and are baptised with poetry and a knowing beyond opinion, fashions and trends. In a time when the mindset we subscribe to has endangered the world, we need a new knowing based on new capacities. And the newest, freshest, most verdant and most promising of capacities are those related to what is creative in us and in the world.

This makes the cultivation of poetic capabilities central rather than peripheral, the leaven that rises the cake rather than the icing put on top of it.

To help this rising is the aim of this book.

GLOSSARY

Some of the names in Taliesin's songs will not be familiar to modern readers. Most of the Celtic names refer to the fourth book of the ***Mabinogion,*** a collection of traditional Welsh stories that also contains The Tale of Taliesin.

Arianrod is the daughter of the Welsh King **Don**. Her brother is the adventurous **Gwdion** mentioned in Talisin's song. **Dylan**, is one of Arianrod's sons, who on account of his association with the element of water is given the epithet *Son of the Wave* or *Son of the Sea.*

The names **Lleon of Lochlin** and the **Cynvelyn** refer to Welsh Kings.

Nimrod and **Absalom** are names connected to Hebrew Lore.

ABOUT THE AUTHOR

Horst Kornberger is an interdisciplinary artist, educator and writer. He is the director of The Writing Connection and a co-director of 'Creativity Consultants Worldwide'.

Horst lectures internationally on themes of creativity, ecology and the use of the imagination as a healing tool. He is the author of the following books:

Global Hive - *bee crisis and compassionate ecology*

The Writer's Passage - *a journey to the sources of creativity*

The Power of Stories - *nurturing children's imagination and consciousness*

The Delphi Project - *collective imagination and its uses*

Taliesin — recovering the poetic self is available as a workshop and seminar. Enquiries: www.thewritingconnection.com.au

More about the author at www.horstkornberger.com
and http://horstkornberger.blogspot.com.au